Olivet U. M. W.
Faith In Action 1973
Christian Global Concerns



# Can Man Care for the Earth?

# Can Man Care for the Earth?

**Edited by**

**Richard L. Heiss**
**Noel F. McInnis**

They have polluted my land with the carcasses of their detestable idols.

—Jeremiah 16:18

ABINGDON PRESS
Nashville
•
New York

CAN MAN CARE FOR THE EARTH?



*ISBN 0-687-04617-3*

*Library of Congress Catalog Card Number: 72-148071*



SET UP, PRINTED, AND BOUND BY THE PARTHENON PRESS, AT NASHVILLE, TENNESSEE, UNITED STATES OF AMERICA

To Earth, Mother of us all
and
To June, Holly, Scott, Joan
Susan, Shari, and Douglas

# Contents

Owed to a Dying Planet . . . . . 9
How to Use This Book . . . . . 12

**Good Neighborhood on Spaceship Earth**

It's a Small World, After All . . . . . 18
Who Is My Neighbor? . . . . . 21
Popullution . . . . . 25
". . . as Yourself" . . . . . 26
"Those Who Are Exclusive Exclude Themselves" . . . . . 29
Whose Neighbor Am I? . . . . . 31

**Man: Caretaker or Undertaker?**

The Meek? . . . . . 36
Self-made Man? . . . . . 36

Who Else? . . . . . 39
Jonah . . . . . 40
Dominion? . . . . . 45
Is Man His Own Doomsday Machine? . . . . . 47
Bottom of the Ninth . . . . 60
Unless We Guard Them Well . . . . 61
The Cancer Called Man . . . . 61

**At-One-Ment: Getting with Spaceship Earth**

Bank Accounts . . . . . 73
Magic Mirrors . . . . . 74
Something Is Right with the Earth . . . . . 76
Something Is Right with You . . . . . 77
"... and It Was Very Good" . . . . . 79
Thinking the World Together . . . . . 79
Powerhouse . . . . . 80
Put Yourself in the Planet's Shoe . . . . . 92
How I Got Radicalized: The Making of an Agitator for Zero . . . . . 95
Undertakings . . . . . 101

**Earth: A New Covenant**

Our Landlord Is a Softy . . . . . 108
Private Property? . . . . . 110
A Tenet for Tenants . . . . . 113
Ten Commandments of the New Earth . . . . . 117
*Will* Man Care for the Earth? . . . . . 118

**Bibliography** . . . . . 121

## Owed to a Dying Planet

This book was initially inspired by four films entitled *Choice: The Imperative of Tomorrow*, which are briefly annotated under "Films" in the concluding bibliography, and which we highly recommend for viewing and discussion in conjunction with this volume.

Like the *Choice* films, our effort is an attempt at prophecy: calling the faithful to their senses before they are doomed as a consequence of transgressing God's laws. The words of Isaiah 24:1-5 are as relevant today as when they were first written, especially those of the fifth verse:

*The earth lies polluted*
*under its inhabitants;*
*for they have transgressed the laws,*
*violated the statutes,*
*broken the everlasting covenant.*

The laws, statutes, and covenant which contemporary man has transgressed are those which govern the functioning of our planet. Mankind presently faces his first scientifically predictable apocalypse. The world may well be close to an end, but not because a supernatural, creaturelike God threatens to smash it in an act of wrathful intervention in human affairs. If Isaiah's prophecy is fulfilled in our time, it will be the consequence of man's local tampering with the physical laws which govern the operation of God's whole creation. More specifically, the ocean's capacity to produce the life-giving oxygen upon which man depends is being decreased, not because God is angry, but because man has polluted it with DDT, garbage, sewage, and overconsumption of sealife. Jeremiah's words are also relevant:

*for my people have committed two*
*evils:*
*they have forsaken me,*
*the fountain of living waters,*
*and hewed out cisterns for them-*
*selves,*
*broken cisterns,*
*that can hold no water. (2:13.)*

The doomsday psychology which pervades much of the current literature on the environmental crisis increases our alienation from "the fountain of living waters." The intent of this book is to acknowledge the fact of an impending environmental doomsday, and to help the reader overcome the psychology of fear and hopelessness which threatens to render such an apocalypse inevitable. While we do not deny the inevitability of ultimate apocalypse, we do not think that the currently impending one is necessary.

Although this book questions man's present ability to care for the earth, we have no doubt concerning his potential capacity to do so. It is our Christian conviction that the gap between man's present abilities and ultimate capabilities can be bridged in time to avoid disaster. Our intention in the following pages is to enable others to perceive the Christian faith as an affirmation that man *can* care for the earth, providing that he does not continue to transgress the laws, violate the statutes, and break the everlasting covenant.

The reader of this book is indebted to numerous persons who helped make it possible: socio-economist Robert Theobald, the Rev. Nordan C. Murphy of the National Council of Churches' Department of Church Renewal, and the Rev. Hilbert J. Berger, Assistant General Secretary of the Board of Laity of The United Methodist Church, who were of invaluable assistance in our initial conception of this volume; the numerous authors and publishers who granted permission to quote or reprint their works; and Sarah Goldman, Sue Watson, Connie Beaugureau, Pat Stolle, and Marilyn Colliver, who typed successive stages of the manuscript over its two-year evolution.

We would like to hear from readers about any projects and programs, local, regional, national, or international, which embody the affirmation that man can care for the earth. Such information, and any other feedback the reader wishes to share, may be addressed to us in care of:

The Center for Curriculum Design
823 Foster Street
Evanston, Illinois 60204

## How to Use This Book

Readers of this book are urged to heed the lesson of the following fable:

Several summers ago there was a Scotty who went to the country for a visit. He decided that all the farm dogs were cowards, because they were afraid of a certain animal that had a white stripe down its back. "You are a pussy-cat and I can lick you," the Scotty said to the farm dog who lived in the house where the Scotty was visiting. "I can lick the little animal with the white stripe, too. Show him to me." "Don't you want to ask any questions about him?" said the farm dog. "Naw," said the Scotty. "*You* ask the questions."

So the farm dog took the Scotty into the woods and showed him the white-striped animal and the Scotty closed in on him, growling and slashing. It was all over in a moment and the Scotty lay on his back. When he came to, the farm dog said, "What happened?" "He threw vitriol," said the Scotty, "but he never laid a glove on me."

A few days later the farm dog told the Scotty there was another animal all the farm dogs were afraid of. "Lead me to him," said the Scotty. "I can lick anything that doesn't wear horseshoes." "Don't you want to ask any questions about him?" said the farm dog. "Naw," said the Scotty. "Just show me where he hangs out." So the farm dog led him to a place in the woods and pointed out the little animal when he came along. "A clown," said the Scotty, "a push-over," and he closed in, leading with his left and exhibiting some mighty fancy footwork. In less than a second the Scotty was flat on his back, and when he woke up the farm dog was pulling quills out of him. "What happened?" said the farm dog. "He pulled a knife on me," said the Scotty, "but at least I have learned how you fight out here in the country, and now I am going to beat *you* up." So he closed in on the farm dog, holding his nose with one front paw to ward off the vitriol and covering his eyes with the other front paw to keep out the knives. The Scotty couldn't see his opponent and he couldn't smell his opponent and he was so badly beaten that he had to be taken back to the city and put in a nursing home.

Moral: It is better to ask some of the questions than to know all the answers.[1]

This book has a specific purpose: to encourage the reader to ask some questions he never asked before. The values of asking new questions are many. New questions help us to enlarge our perspective and deepen our experiences of life. They help us to seek new, more inclusive answers to our problems. They help us to find new purpose in our existence. They renew our everyday being. They help us to mean, rather than merely exist.

This book also has a specific limitation: it provides no answers. The book will be read by unique individuals, and the questions it raises require answers that are unique to each individual's experience. If we attempted to provide answers, some of them would be to questions the reader never asked. We would be depriving the reader of the joy of learning: found answers are always more rewarding and exciting than given ones.

The following pages contain numerous quotations

[1] James Thurber, "The Scotty Who Knew Too Much." Copyright © 1940, James Thurber. Copyright © 1968, Helen Thurber. From *Fables for Our Time*, published by Harper & Row. Originally printed in *The New Yorker*.

and articles, interlinked with questions. The questions are derived from the implications of the previous materials, and often serve additionally as a preview of the material immediately following. The quotations and articles can be read quite rapidly. The questions are not meant for merely reading, however. *They are to be thought about at length!* If the reader takes this book seriously, he will find himself enlarging the fundamental meaning of his faith, and this is not done quickly.

We do not look upon this as our book, but as *your* book. Thus it is designed to get you involved, to encourage you to think through for yourself the many relationships among the materials presented. If you will continually refer back to previously read pages, skipping around freely as the overall "territory" of the book becomes familiar to you, you will undoubtedly see relationships which have not even occurred to us. It is thus that you will, indeed, make it *your* book.

We are hopeful that this book will be widely used in discussion groups, because its value as a stimulus to fresh thought will be greatly enhanced by a sharing of responses. Those who, individually or as a group, wish to further pursue the questions raised in the following pages will find a helpful guide to filmed and printed materials in the concluding bibliography.

Our honeymoon with the
planet is over.
We must take our marriage
to the earth seriously.
We can't divorce it
—*but it can divorce us!*

# Good Neighborhood on Spaceship Earth

Many people these days wonder what it is like to be on a spaceship. They don't realize that they *are* on a spaceship. Man has been on a spaceship all this time. It is a tiny little spaceship, only 8,000 miles in diameter. It is also a fantastically lonely little spaceship. The nearest star is 92 million miles away, and the next nearest star is so remote that it takes two and one-half years for its light to come to us. And yet this tiny spaceship is so superbly designed that it provides everything man needs for his journey through space.

—R. Buckminster Fuller

## It's a Small World, After All

Mankind is about to discover another planet. Until recently it was assumed that we had discovered all the planets in our solar system, but it now turns out that this is not the case. In the process of scanning the skies for Mercury, Venus, Mars, Jupiter, Saturn, Uranus, Neptune, and Pluto, we overlooked the most important planet of all—Earth. Earth is the most important planet by any human definition, since this is the planet which sustains human life. And it is precisely because Earth is our home that we never discovered it before.

Man-on-earth is in the same predicament as fish in the water. "If you want to know about water," Marshall McLuhan has quipped *ad infinitum,* "don't ask a fish." The environment into which we are born remains invisible to us unless one of two things happens: (1) we leave it, or (2) it changes drastically. Quite recently both these things have happened to man-on-earth. Man left the earth long enough to look it over, and brought back pictures which make it difficult for us to overlook the planet any longer. And those of us who stayed on earth discovered our planet by virtue of the fact that its feedback is doing things to us which were entirely unintended in our doings to it. The coincidence of these events is quite literally leading to our belated discovery of the third planet from our sun. What we are discovering, of course, is that the planet as a whole behaves differently than its parts. Our present habits of relating to the planet only in part are producing a planetary reaction which, on the whole, will be unfavorable to our continued enjoyment of the planet if not our very existence itself.

We are discovering, in other words, that our planet is a spaceship, *a closed, finite system in which all be-*

*haviors ultimately feed back through the system upon themselves.* Inappropriate behavior in one component of the system can disrupt or destroy the entire system. If the system is as complex as that of our planet, the destruction is likely to be relative: the source of disruption will probably be eliminated by the system long before the system itself collapses. The system will become greatly altered in the process, but the whole will still survive the loss of some parts.

On a spaceship every subsystem is related to every other subsystem. Nothing functions without reference to everything else. All subsystems are affected by a major change in any one of them. In other words, the various subsystems of a spaceship constitute one unified, balanced overall system. Any imbalance originating in one of the subsystems is eventually redressed throughout the whole.

So well integrated are our planet's numerous systems that the earth functions as a single organism. This fact we have demonstrated to ourselves most drastically by the massive application of fertilizers and pesticides. The system-disruption potentials of this activity are most vividly illustrated by our long-term experience with DDT. DDT symbolizes our dread of an unavoidable function of the planet, that of death. Although DDT's effects are mild in comparison with many other chemicals used in our death-control tactics, it has become the focus of all those who see the folly of avoiding our death by annihilating other forms of life.

DDT is being metabolized by the entire planet. It is found in the fatty tissue of penguins at the South Pole, thousands of miles from its nearest application. DDT is found in the fatty tissues of creatures of the air, creatures of the mountain, creatures of the plains, and creatures of the mid-ocean. DDT is carried by all the planet's transmission systems—air, water, and food chains. As a result, the planet is soaking up DDT like a sponge. When DDT begins, as it has, to take its toll of the oceanic vegetation which produces 70 percent of the earth's atmospheric oxygen, it definitely tolls for thee. Since we are at the top of the food chain, we humans stand to concentrate more DDT in our systems than any other species. The concentration of DDT in our species is already so great that the milk of nursing mothers, in this country at least, exceeds two to six times the amount of DDT considered adequate to make milk unfit for commercial sale (i.e., human consumption).

On a spaceship all inappropriate behaviors ultimately feed back through the system to their source. When we cast our dread upon the waters, we can be sure of its eventual return.

### *For God so loved the world . . . (John 3:16)*

*Does God care for our planet? What does it mean to care for something? What evidence is there, in addition to John 3:16, that God cares for the world?*

*What does the statement "for God so loved the world" tell us about God? About the earth? Does it tell us something about our relationship with the planet?*

*What would it mean for us to love the earth? Does the planet look like man loves it? How would it be different if it had man's love?*

*Can the earth get along without our care? Does a better planet depend on us?*

*How would you express the phrase "for God so loved the world" without using the words "God," "love," or "world"?*

*Does God accept the world or reject it? How can we*

*know? Must we accept the world? What price do we pay for accepting the world? What price do we pay for not accepting the world? Is God's acceptance of the world conditional, i.e. qualified in any way? Is our acceptance of the world conditional?*

See Paul Tillich's sermon "You Are Accepted," in *The Shaking of the Foundations* (New York: Scribner's, 1948).

## Who Is My Neighbor? (Luke 10:29-37)

*The following piece was written in 1937, to point out the absurdity of* exclusive *Americanism by illustrating the global interdependence of culture. Its demonstration that Americanism is an* inclusive *concept is more pertinent today than ever.*

There can be no question about the average American's Americanism or his desire to preserve this precious heritage at all costs. Nevertheless, some insidious foreign ideas have already wormed their way into his civilization without his realizing what was going on. Thus dawn finds the unsuspecting patriot garbed in pajamas, a garment of East Indian origin; and lying in a bed built on a pattern which originated in either Persia or Asia Minor. He is muffed to the ears in un-American materials; cotton, first domesticated in India; linen, domesticated in the Near East; wool from an animal native to Asia Minor; or silk whose uses were first discovered by the Chinese. All these substances have been transformed into cloth by methods invented in Southwestern Asia. If the weather is cold enough he may even be sleeping under an eiderdown quilt invented in Scandinavia.

On awakening he glances at the clock, a medieval European invention, uses one potent Latin word in abbreviated form, rises in haste, and goes to the bathroom. Here, if he stops to think about it, he must feel himself in the presence of a great American institution: he will have heard stories of both the quality and frequency of foreign plumbing and will know that in no other country does the average man perform his ablutions in the midst of such splendor. But the insidious foreign influence pursues him even here. Glass was invented by the ancient Egyptians, the use of glazed tiles for floors and walls in the Near East, porcelain in China and the art of enameling on metal by Mediterranean artisans of the Bronze Age. Even his bathtub and toilet are but slightly modified copies of Roman originals. The only purely American contribution to the ensemble is the steam radiator, against which our patriot very briefly and unintentionally places his posterior.

In this bathroom, the American washes with soap invented by the ancient Gauls. Next he cleans his teeth, a subversive European practice which did not invade America until the latter part of the eighteenth century. He then shaves, a masochistic rite first developed by the heathen priests of ancient Egypt and Sumer. The process is made less of a penance by the fact that his razor is of steel, an iron-carbon alloy discovered in either India or Turkestan. Lastly he dries himself on a Turkish towel.

Returning to the bedroom, the unconscious victim of un-American practices removes his clothes from a chair, invented in the Near East; and proceeds to dress. He puts on close-fitting tailored garments whose form derived from the skin clothing of the ancient nomad of the Asiatic steppes and fastens them with buttons whose prototypes appeared in Europe at the close of the Stone

Age. This costume is appropriate enough for outdoor exercise in a cold climate, but is quite unsuited to American summers, steam-heated houses, and Pullmans. Nevertheless, foreign ideas and habits hold the unfortunate man in thrall even when common sense tells him that the authentically American costume of gee string and moccasins would be far more comfortable. He puts on his feet stiff coverings made from hide prepared by a process invented in ancient Egypt and cut to a pattern which can be traced back to ancient Greece, and makes sure that they are properly polished, also a Greek idea. Lastly, he ties about his neck a strip of bright-colored cloth which is a vestigial survival of the shoulder shawls worn by seventh-century Croats. He gives himself a final appraisal in the mirror, an old Mediterranean invention, and goes downstairs to eat breakfast.

Here a whole new series of foreign things confronts him. His food and drink are placed before him in pottery vessels, the popular name of which—china—is sufficient evidence of their origin. His fork is a medieval Italian invention and his spoon a copy of a Roman original. He will usually begin the meal with coffee, an Abyssinian plant first discovered by the Arabs. The American is quite likely to need it to dispel the morning-after effects of overindulgence in fermented drinks, invented in the Near East; or distilled ones, invented by the alchemists of medieval Europe. Whereas the Arabs took their coffee straight, he will probably sweeten it with sugar, discovered in India; and dilute it with cream, both the domestication of cattle and the technique of milking having originated in Asia Minor.

If our patriot is old-fashioned enough to adhere to the so-called American breakfast, his coffee will be accompanied by an orange, domesticated in the Mediterranean region, cantaloupe domesticated in Persia, or grapes domesticated in Asia Minor. He will follow this with a bowl of cereal made from grain domesticated in the Near East and prepared by methods also invented there. From this he will go on to waffles, a Scandinavian invention, with plenty of butter, originally a Near-Eastern cosmetic. As a side dish he may have the egg of a bird domesticated in Southeastern Asia or strips of the flesh of an animal domesticated in the same region, which have been salted and smoked by a process invented in Northern Europe.

Breakfast over, he places upon his head a molded piece of felt, invented by the nomads of Eastern Asia, and if it looks like rain, puts on outer shoes of rubber, discovered by the ancient Mexicans, and takes an umbrella, invented in India. He then sprints for his train—the train, not the sprinting, being an English invention. At the station he pauses for a moment to buy a newspaper, paying for it with coins invented in ancient Lydia. Once aboard he settles back to inhale the fumes of a cigarette invented in Mexico, or a cigar invented in Brazil. Meanwhile, he reads the news of the day, imprinted in characters invented by the ancient Semites by a process invented in Germany upon a material invented in China. As he scans the latest editorial pointing out the dire results to our institutions of accepting foreign ideas, he will not fail to thank a Hebrew God in an Indo-European language that he is one hundred per cent (decimal system invented by the Greeks) American (from Americus Vespucci, Italian geographer).[1]

*We are inevitably bound, for any foreseeable future, to this planet. We may be able to get off it for days at a*

[1] Ralph Linton, "One Hundred Per Cent American," *American Mercury,* April, 1937.

*time, but we must take with us the oxygen and food and water we need to survive.*

*And eventually, we must return.*

—Stewart L. Udall

*Who is my neighbor? Can I avoid him? (Matthew 25:31-46)*

*Can I avoid the consequences of his decisions? (Matthew 5:23-24)*

*Can he avoid the consequences of my decisions? Can either of us fulfill his life without regard to the consequences of the other's actions? (Romans 12:3-5)*

## Popullution

Air pollution is caused by people.

From the time we get up in the morning until we go to bed at night most of the things we do and the things we use cause or have caused air pollution. We get up in the morning and turn on the lights; much of our electricity is generated by burning fuels and burning causes air pollution. We take a hot shower in water heated by burning gas. Our breakfast is cooked on a stove which uses fuel. The food itself gives off particles and gases into the air, as the fan on the kitchen vent will attest. The food may well have come from land which had been cleared by burning. We get into our car and drive to work; the automobile accounts for over half of our air pollution.

And if the things we use don't contribute directly to air pollution the chances are good that somewhere in their manufacturing process they were smelted, heated, abraded, ground, polished, sanded, or welded, etc., all of which contribute to air pollution. And when we are finished with the object and throw it out, it will probably be burned.[2]

*If my neighbor is defined as anyone whose actions affect me or who is affected by my actions, who, then, on Spaceship Earth is* not *my neighbor?*

## ". . . as Yourself" (Mark 12:31)

Man cannot live without answering the question, "What am I?" The answers to this question may indeed be various, for one man can play a great many different roles, especially in a complex society. He may say in answer to this question, I am a husband, or a father, or a blacksmith, or a Baptist, or an American. Each of these identities corresponds to certain aspects of his life. Rarely in the present age will he say, "I am a human being"; for the human identity as yet is only latent in mankind. This is mainly because there is no clearly identifiable mode of thought and behavior which is associated with it. If a man says, "I am a father," this means that he concerns himself with his children in innumerable ways. If he says, "I am an American," this means that he votes, concerns himself with political affairs, and so on. If he says, "I am a human being," there is no clear activity which corresponds to this identity, mainly because there is no organizational structure which can express such activity. Every identity has to be embodied in an organization; that of a father and a husband, a wife and a mother, in the family; that of an occupation in an occupational organization such as a firm or a university; that of a citizen in a government. It is only mankind that

[2] Bay Area Air Pollution Control District, "Air Pollution and the San Francisco Bay Area" (San Francisco, 1969), p. 2.

remains without any protective shell of organization within which the human identity can function. The United Nations is the beginning of this, and it deserves a great deal of legitimacy, in spite of its minute size and relative impotence, because it does symbolize, however imperfectly, the human identity. It is this creation of the human identity, however, which is the major problem of the Spaceship Earth. The crew of a spaceship must identify with the whole enterprise; otherwise there will be a shipwreck.

One of the great obstacles towards the realization of the human identity is the fear that taking on the human identity will destroy our other identities, especially our national and religious identities. This fear is only valid if the other identities demand unconditional loyalty. If we demand unconditional loyalty to our family, we obviously cannot have a wholly satisfactory identity as a citizen, for the larger identity may occasionally demand sacrifice of the smaller. Similarly, if we are to establish the human identity, we must abandon unconditional loyalty either to the national or to the religious identity. This does not mean, however, that we give up these identities; rather does it mean that we redeem them in the promise of the larger and the truer identity. This act of redemption, both of nationalism and of religion, may not be easy. It is, however, an act of redemption and not of destruction. As Jesus himself says, "I come not to destroy but to fulfill"; and the larger identity does not destroy but fulfills the lesser identity. An unconditional loyalty, either to the family or the church or the nation, will in the long run destroy that to which we are committed. The Christian Church has always maintained that unconditional loyalty, either to the family or the church or the nation, will in the long run destroy even that to which we are committed. The Christian Church has always maintained that the only unconditional loyalty was to God himself. This is a doctrine which must be continually refreshed, reinterpreted, and rediscovered; and it is one of utmost importance for mankind in the critical days which lie ahead.

What this means in practice, both in our identity as citizens of a nation and as members of a church, is that we are going to have to learn to be particular and to abandon our claims for universality. No nation, no church, and no ideology is going to conquer the earth. Each nation and each church is going to have to learn to live as something particular in the midst of a larger universe. Jesus may indeed "reign where'er the sun doth his successive journeys run," but he will reign only in the hearts of those whom he has called, and they will have neither the right nor the will to impose his reign on others. As imperialism is being abandoned in the national sphere, so that each nation will reign only over its home territory, so we must come to the abandonment of imperialism in the religious sphere too. This does not mean the end of missionary effort, nor the end of proclaiming the Gospel. It must be proclaimed, however, in a way that says, "He that hath ears to hear, let him hear." In these days even the Roman Catholic Church has had to come to terms with the fact that it is indeed a sect, however large and powerful; and it is preparing for peaceful coexistence, even with the secular religion of Communism. Many Protestants, oddly enough, are far behind the Roman Church in their recognition, however unpalatable the fact may be, of this necessity of the twentieth century. Americans are still less ready to recognize their particularity and "smallness"; the grandiose illusions of being not only "a" but "the" great power are still luring them on to destruction, and at the moment in regard to Viet-Nam, they seem to be seized by a national madness and paranoid delusions of grandeur.[3]

*If the crew of Spaceship Earth must identify with the whole enterprise, how do I reconcile differences which divide me from my neighbor? Is it the differences which divide us, or is it our attitudes toward our differences which divide us?*

## "Those Who Are Exclusive Exclude Themselves." (Emerson)

Emerson's earlier countryman, Benjamin Franklin, illustrated this truth with a parable written in biblical style. He entitled it "A Parable Against Persecution."

1. And it came to pass after these things, that Abraham sat in the door of his tent, about the going down of the sun.

2. And behold a man, bent with age, coming from the way of the wilderness, leaning on a staff.

3. And Abraham arose and met him, and said unto him, Turn in, I pray thee, and wash thy feet, and tarry all night, and thou shalt arise early in the morning, and go on thy way.

4. But the man said, Nay, for I will abide under this tree.

5. And Abraham pressed him greatly; so he turned, and they went into the tent; and Abraham baked unleavened bread, and they did eat.

[3] From Kenneth E. Boulding, "The Wisdom of Man and the Wisdom of God," *Human Values on the Spaceship Earth,* published by Council Press for the Commission on Church and Economic Life, National Council of Churches in the U.S.A. Copyright © 1966. Used with permission.

6. And when Abraham saw that the man blest not God, he said unto him, Wherefore dost thou not worship the most high God, Creator of heaven and earth?

7. And the man answered and said, I do not worship thy God, neither do I call upon his name; for I have made to myself a god, which abideth always in mine house, and provideth me with all things.

8. And Abraham's zeal was kindled against the man, and he arose and fell upon him, and drove him forth with blows into the wilderness.

9. And God called unto Abraham, saying, Abraham, where is the stranger?

10. And Abraham answered and said, Lord, he would not worship thee, neither would he call upon thy name; therefore have I driven him out from before my face into the wilderness.

11. And God said, Have I borne with him these hundred and ninety and eight years, and nourished him, and clothed him, not withstanding his rebellion against me; and couldst not thou, who art thyself a sinner, bear with him one night?

12. And Abraham said, Let not the anger of the Lord wax hot against his servant; lo, I have sinned; lo, I have sinned; forgive me, I pray thee.

13. And Abraham arose, and went forth into the wilderness, and sought diligently for the man, and found him, and returned with him to the tent; and when he had entreated him kindly, he sent him away on the morrow with gifts.

14. And God spake again unto Abraham, saying, For this thy sin shall thy seed be afflicted four hundred years in a strange land;

15. But for thy repentance will I deliver them; and they shall come forth with power, and with gladness of heart, and with much substance.

## *Dramatizing the Parable Against Persecution*

*The preceding parable is acted out daily in the life of the church. This can be dramatized by the following exercise in role-playing:*

*Assume that Abraham represents the church, that the man from the wilderness represents the secular world, and that God—as always—represents God. The church and the secular world each speak with several voices. God, of course, speaks with one voice.*

*Therefore, for the role of Abraham (the church) let one person represent that voice of the church which is concerned with personal salvation; let another person represent that voice of the church which is concerned with the world's ills; and let another person represent that voice of the church which is concerned with its own perpetuation.*

*For the role of the man in the wilderness (secular world), let one or more persons represent reliance on the god of political/social/economic control; and let one or more persons represent reliance on the god of technological progress.*

*For the role of God, let one person represent the voice of God.*

*Now, reenact the parable against persecution.*

*Question: From what does the church become excluded in the enactment of its various voices?*

# Whose Neighbor Am I?

Imagine that we could compress the world's present population of over three billion persons into one town of 1,000 persons, in exactly the same proportions. In such a town of 1,000 persons there would be only 70

(United States) Americans. These 70 Americans—a mere 7 percent of the town's population—would receive half the town's income. This would be the direct result of their monopolizing over half the town's available material resources.[4]

The 70 Americans would have an average life expectancy of 70 years. The other 930 would average less than 40 years. The lowest income group among the Americans, even though it included a few people who were hungry much of the time, would be better off by far than the average of the other townsmen. The 70 Americans and about 200 others representing Western Europe, and a few classes in South America, South Africa, Australia, and Japan, would be well off by comparison with the rest.

Could such a town, in which the 930 non-Americans were quite aware of both the fact and means of the Americans' advantages, survive? Could the 70 Americans continue to extract the majority of the raw materials essential to their standard of living from the property of the other 930 inhabitants? While doing so, could they convince the other 930 inhabitants to limit their population growth on the thesis that resources are limited? How many of the 70 Americans would have to become soldiers? How much of their material and human resources would have to be devoted to military efforts in order to keep the rest of the town at its present disadvantage?

Chances are the 70 Americans would have to organize into a military camp in order to maintain their material dominance of the remainder of the town. Chances are most of the Americans would be too insecure or guilty

[4] Paul Ehrlich, *The Population Bomb* (New York: Ballantine Books, 1969), p. 133.

about their situation to enjoy their dominance. Chances are this guilt and insecurity would lead some of the Americans to protest the situation and call for a change. Chances are that the protesting Americans would find themselves subjected to variations of the same repressive forces being used to subdue the other 930 townspeople. Chances are the military camp would also be a police camp.

The most regretful thing about the situation you have been asked to imagine is that it is not imaginary. For such is the present material relationship and incipient political relationship of the United States to the rest of the world. The material relationship is very clear: the United States is systematically plundering the planet's physical resources. And if the political conclusions drawn above are not yet so, they are rapidly becoming so. The logical complement of a nation of plunderers is a nation of police.

*Since so many of our global neighbors perceive us in the above terms (whether accurately or not), how are we to avoid the following judgment on our spaceship?*

*"And if a house is divided against itself,*
*that house will not be able to stand." (Mark 3:25)*

# Man: Caretaker Or Undertaker?

Then God said, "Let us make man in our image, after our likeness; and let them have dominion over the fish of the sea, and over the birds of the air, and over the cattle, and over all the earth, and over every creeping thing that creeps upon the earth."

—Genesis 1:26

(See also Psalm 8:3-8)

And I brought you into a plentiful land
to enjoy its fruits and its good things.
But when you came in you defiled my land,
and made my heritage an abomination.

—Jeremiah 2:7

## The Meek?

Man has inherited the earth, and the ordeal of change is everywhere. The age of mammals, which endured in all its splendor for one hundred million years, has given way to the age of man. For the first time in the history of the planet a single species dominates all, for better or for worse. Moreover, this dominance has been attained during the last minute of evolutionary time, and the shambles is evident. Now, in the last second, so to speak, we have plucked the fruit of the tree of knowledge, and nothing will ever be the same again. The immortals were mortal after all. The moon goddess, the goddess of love, and the red god of war are no longer to be worshiped in the heavens but have become dead planets toward which we aim our missiles. In the laboratory man assumes even the mantle of the Creator Himself and aims at the creation of life. Presumptuous, magnificent, or foolish, or all of them together, this is our time, if only for a moment in eternity. It is dangerous, exhilarating, tragic and portentous, for we have a tiger by the tail.[1]

*Does man's creation in the image of God mean that man is godlike? Is Creation the absolute domain of God?*

*Has God's creative process ceased, or is it continuous? Does man participate in God's creative process?*

*Have powers traditionally attributed to God become man's possession?*

## Self-made Man?

Of all the variations that might be played upon the theme of human procreation, the ultimate—at least,

[1] N. J. Berrill, *Inherit the Earth* (New York: Fawcett Premier Books, 1967), p. 7.

the "ultimate" we can now project—will be the production of beings whose specifications can be drawn in advance. This could come about, scientists predict, through the manipulation of the genetic material itself, though the estimates of when this might come to pass vary considerably.

The basic genetic material, the stuff of which chromosomes are made, is dexoyribonucleic acid or DNA. In the coiled structure of the DNA molecule and the complex arrangement of its atoms lie the final secrets of heredity. DNA's genetic messages are written out in a four-letter code, each "letter" being a specific chemical substance. Scientists have begun to be able to read the genetic code—but only in a halting, incipient way, and it may take a long time before they become really fluent readers. But once we can read, we may then learn to "write"—i.e., to give genetic instructions—in the DNA code.

When that time comes, man's powers will be truly godlike. He may bring into being creatures never before seen or imagined in the universe. He may even choose to create new forms of humanity—beings that might be better adapted to survive on the surface of Jupiter, or at the bottom of the Atlantic Ocean.

Even without going that far, man presumably will be able to write out any set of specifications he might desire for his ideal human being. This is what many scientists mean when they talk about man controlling his own evolution. And who can find fault with that? Is there anyone not in favor of emphasizing man's good qualities and eliminating the bad ones? The rub, of course, is that "good" and "bad" are words that are easier to say than to apply.

There is at least one area of consensus as to what is good for man—the medical area. Most people would agree that it is good to reduce infant mortality, to make it possible for infertile parents to have children, to eradicate cancer and heart disease.

But consensus is not unanimity. Dissident voices are even now insisting that many of our so-called medical advances actually militate against human progress by aggravating the population problem, thus assuring an overcrowded planet where more people will die of war and starvation. Others warn of the deterioration of the human race because so many people with hereditary defects—people who formerly would have died at an early age—are now being kept alive, to marry and pass on their defects. A majority undoubtedly would choose—at least for themselves and those they love—the benefits of health and longevity and worry later about problems like overpopulation and the possible deterioration of the race.

Beyond getting rid of diseases and defects, there is the prospect that we can actually improve human beings—making them more intelligent, more talented, more virtuous—by manipulating genetic material. No one would argue that man couldn't stand some improvement, but having the actual power to do so presents some sticky choices. Who is it that we will appoint to play God for us? Which scientist, which statesman, artist, judge, poet, theologian, philosopher, educator—of which nation, race, or creed—will you trust to write the specifications, to decide which characteristics are desirable and which not? [2]

[2] From "The New Man: What Will He Be Like?" by Albert Rosenfeld, *Life* magazine, October 1, 1965, © 1965, Time Inc.

## Who Else?

O God,
When the world stops
and no man is constrained to ask why,
who will convene the court,
arrange the formula,
call the roll of scholars,
find the star?
Will we always be Pilates
washing our hands?
Amen.[3]

*When we assume a role in the process of Creation, do we need to revise our concept of God?*

[3] Warren Lane Molton, *Bruised Reeds* (Valley Forge: Judson Press, 1970), p. 8. Used by permission.

## Jonah

When God looked for Jonah, he couldn't see him for the dust. When God called to Jonah, Jonah didn't hear him for the wind which was whistling in his ears.

Jonah ran to the end of the land, as far as he could go, and when he reached the end of the land and came to the edge of the sea, he took a boat.

"Do you have a reservation?" they asked him.

"No," said Jonah, because he never had time to plan ahead.

But there was one ticket left and Jonah thought he was lucky to get it, even though they charged him an exorbitant price.

Picture him at the customs, Jonah with the guilty face. Any number of crooks and smugglers had gone on board without raising any suspicion at all. But Jonah was subjected to the closest search and questioning. They made him undo the knots in all the string around his suitcases (he hadn't been able to locate the key) and empty the unwieldly paper bags in which he'd thrown his last-minute things.

Lord, what a muddle Jonah's luggage was in! He'd forgotten his toothbrush and his shaving kit. But, on the other hand, the bottom of his grip was full of old photographs and theater programs that he couldn't bear to throw away. There were photographs of several sweethearts he had very nearly married. One girl he had run after for years, but she had never given him a tumble. The reason he had this bric-a-brac with him when he reached the edge of the sea was very simply this: he didn't know how long he'd be away. He didn't even know if he was coming back.

When Jonah finally stumbled up the gangplank and on board, he immediately went down to his stateroom, locked the door, and fell onto his berth. It was only when the engines started to turn over and his staring eyes saw upon the white ceiling the dancing reflection of fast-moving water that Jonah's fists at last unclenched, and the sweat on his brow dried up. The peace and contentment which most people feel when they are beside their own hearth was experienced by Jonah only when he was on a journey. All his deepest reading and thinking had ever been done on moving vehicles. As soon as he stopped moving he felt hemmed in. And even when he got a bit used to his moving surroundings—as soon as a bare stateroom began to take on the contours of him and habit, for instance—as soon as that happened, the unease came back to Jonah like a vulture.

So within his little locked cabin, lying with his face pressed down into his pillow, Jonah tried to hold onto the feeling of relief which came to him with the beginning of a journey. And his stomach felt the queasy rocking of the boat, and he lay listening to the creaking of all the ship boards and the rushing of the sailors to and fro.

"There's someone guilty on board," said the sailors when the storm arose.

"That's me," thought Jonah without a second thought. That's the sort of egotist he was. He didn't give a thought to all the crooks and smugglers on the passenger list. He didn't consider the cutthroats in the crew who had signed up to get away from the scene of their crimes. No, Jonah had this guiltier-than-thou attitude, and all that he could think of was Jonah.

He opened the door of his stateroom and he said:

"Here I am, boys."

The sailors picked him up (he had asked for it) and swung him by his arms and legs, one, two, three, and yo-heave-ho, and over he went. Splash! And into the jaws of the whale.

And in the belly of the whale, where it was warm and enclosed, and where it was physically impossible to run any farther, Jonah gave up.

Jonah cried out to the Lord. And this time Jonah's words weren't the panting, incoherent snatches of a man running away from his fear. This time it was despair; but it was his own despair. And for the first time he cried out with his own voice.

In the belly of the whale, Jonah was transformed. He reversed all his behavior patterns. People who had known Jonah before, and met him after the whale, said: "Jonah, you're a changed man."

It wasn't that his hair had turned white or anything obvious like that. It was simply that everything he had done before, he now did in reverse. He had been a fearful man and he had suddenly changed into an angry man. As precipitately as he'd run away from Nineveh, he now wanted to dash toward it. Just as sharply as he'd turned away from God's word, he now wanted to overdo God's word.

"Hey, son!" shouted God.

"I'm off to Nineveh," yelled Jonah. "Don't stop me."

"Wait a minute," said God, trying to keep up with him. "What are you going to do when you get there?"

"Fire a burst!" replied Jonah.

"Now take it easy," said the Lord, and he held Jonah back by his shirttail.

"But they don't listen to YOUR WORD," stormed Jonah. "We're not going to stand for that, are we?"

So the Lord made him sit down and cool off under a gourd. As if in a speeded-up, documentary movie, Jonah saw it sprout from seed, flower, and then, to his consternation, it withered before its time.

"What's the big idea?" he protested.

"Look," said the Lord. "Don't you go getting sentimental over the life and death of a gourd. This happens to be one of the stiffest, prickliest, least organized of all the organisms in my vegetable kingdom. Whereas people, and this includes even the people of Nineveh, are the most highly organized of all my organisms. Where's your sense of proportion, son?"

Then Jonah understood.

His fear and anger fell away from him, like so much unnecessary luggage, jettisoned. And this left room for love of the whole of creation to well up in him. And he was no longer angry with Nineveh, which had after all represented nothing to him but his own past. Instead of a turreted town crammed with phantasmagoria, it now appeared before him as a plain, ordinary, workaday city, and the people in it were only people, after all.

Imagine Jonah now, having left behind his luggage of confusion and turmoil. Free-riding and life-accepting, as he walked along the road to Nineveh. Simplicity was in his pocket, and the principle of the gourd was deep-rooted in his heart.

Without knowing the scientific details, he knew he was a man who had come out of the sea. And he knew he was a man who had come out of the sun. The Lord had told him all this when he said:

"Consider the gourd. Respect it."

Because Jonah still thought things out best when he was walking, he had a long, calm discussion with the Lord on the way to Nineveh.

"If you created the seed and the life and the sprouting," Jonah asked, "why did you create the negating and rejecting? The fear and the anger and the running away?"

"To tell you the truth," said God, "I had no idea it was going to go this far. Of all the roads it might have taken, this is surely the most surprising. When I was in the infinitesimal speck which held the potentiality of creation, how was I to know that it would expand to become the universe? And when I blazed and exploded in the innumerable suns, how could I foresee that out of the near collision of two of them would leap the tide which would cool into planets? This by the way," said God confidentially, "I learned from Sir James Jeans. Most of what I know comes from Albert Einstein. Before that I had only Newton to go on. And before that . . ."

"But before Man?" asked Jonah, shocked out of his wits. "Do you mean you understood nothing at all? Didn't you exist?"

"Certainly," said God patiently. "I have told you how I exploded in the stars. Then I drifted for aeons in clouds of inchoate gas. As matter stabilized, I acquired the knowledge of valency. When matter cooled, I lay sleeping in the insentient rocks. After that I floated fecund in the unconscious seaweed upon the faces of the deep. Later I existed in the stretching paw of the tiger and the blinking eye of the owl. Each form of knowledge led to the more developed next. Organic matter led to sentience which led to consciousness which led inevitably to my divinity."

"And what will you become next?" asked Jonah.

"I don't know," said God reverently. "I am waiting to be told."

"By whom?" asked Jonah, and he looked around the lonely landscape in dismay.

"How I tremble," sang God. "In rapture before the next stroke of consciousness! How I yearn to be created further!"

"But I don't like this at all," cried Jonah. "Can't we

go back to the way it used to be? You scared me to death most of the time. But how I loved to hear your scolding voice."

"I couldn't go on forever," said God severely, "telling tall stories about whales, any more than I could have remained inert once the first colloidal systems started to form or inchoate once the form of the atom was established."

"But it was cozy," sobbed Jonah. "You and me; I and thou."

"Now it shall be We are One."

"And shall I never call you father any more? And will I never hear you call me son again?" asked Jonah.

"You may call me," said God agreeably, "anything you please. Would you like to discuss semantics?"

So Jonah found himself alone on the road to Nineveh. And yet he was not alone. For the gourd was with him, and the lungfish, and the stars. He knew that he was a man who had come out of the sea. And he knew that he was a man who had come out of the sun. And in Nineveh he took root, and he flowered in the expression of his consciousness until he died.[4]

*Is man the Creation's way of becoming conscious of itself?*

## Dominion?

*When we assume a role in the process of Creation, do we need to rethink the nature of our faith?*

[4] Irene Orgel, "Jonah." Chicago: The Ecumenical Institute, mimeographed.

What did Christianity tell people about their relations with the environment? . . . By gradual stages a loving and all-powerful God had created light and darkness, the heavenly bodies, the earth and all its planets, animals, birds and fishes. Finally, God had created Adam and, as an afterthought, Eve to keep man from being lonely. Man named all the animals, thus establishing his dominance over them. God planned all of this explicitly for man's benefit and rule: no item in the physical creation had any purpose save to serve man's purposes. And, although man's body is made of clay, he is not simply part of nature: he is made in God's image. . . . Christianity not only established a dualism of man and nature but also insisted that it is God's will that man exploit nature for his proper ends. . . . Christianity made it possible to exploit nature in a mood of indifference to the feelings of natural objects. . . . We shall continue to have a worsening ecologic crisis until we reject the Christian axiom that nature has no reason for existence save to serve man. . . . Both our present science and our present technology are so tinctured with orthodox Christian arrogance toward nature that no solution for ecologic crises can be expected from them alone. Since the roots of our troubles are so largely religious, the remedy must be also essentially religious, whether we call it that or not. We must rethink and refeel our nature and destiny.[5]

*What does it* really *mean to have dominion over God's works? Does it mean dominance of God's Creation? If so, what becomes of God's relationship to the Creation? If not, then what* is *the nature of our relationship to God's Creation?*

[5] Lynn White, "The Historic Roots of Our Ecological Crisis," *Science*, March 10, 1967. Copyright 1967 by the American Association for the Advancement of Science.

## Is Man His Own Doomsday Machine?

*Remember the good old days, when only God could end the world?*

Man has inadvertently set into motion a global doomsday mechanism which many scientists fear could end much of the life on our planet.

His handiwork, done in the name of scientific and technological progress, can make the earth shake, cause rain to fall, clouds to form, snuff the breath out of the great trade winds, alter the oceans, add potentially harmful chemicals to his food chain, cook the Great Lakes, and change the world's climate—all unintentionally.

For the first time in history, man's activities are beginning to upset the balance of nature on a worldwide scale. Scientists are becoming alarmed. The things man has wrought are reaching the proportions of titanic natural catastrophes.

"Man has made a miserable mess of the world in which he lives," says Dr. W. Frank Blair, zoology professor at the University of Texas in Houston and director of the United States participation in the International Biological Program, an effort to find out what living things are being threatened and how to save them. Including man.

"Time is running out on the opportunity to reverse the trend so that we may maintain what environmental quality there is left and, hopefully, regain some lost ground," Dr. Blair adds.

Although the detrimental effects of air and water pollution and radioactive fallout on humans are well appreciated, the growing concern now is that the environmental changes may trigger some irreversible effects in the thin band of air, water, and land that supports life. The changes, it is feared, could leave a dry, cold, and relatively lifeless planet for future generations of human beings.

Man has become an endangered species. Unlike the lion, whooping crane, and rhinoceros, which face extinction at the hands of man, the danger to the human race results from three great man-made threats—nuclear war, overpopulation, and environmental changes.

Some of these critical environmental changes have already been felt. Chicago has more rainfall and thunderstorms than surrounding areas because of the city's urban pollution. The same is true for St. Louis and some other metropolitan areas.

Communities downwind from the Chicago-Gary industrial complex get more rain and hail because of the air pollution that drifts over from their neighboring giants. The recent earthquake centered in southern Illinois and felt throughout the midwest may have, at least in part, been triggered by man's activities.

As the problems become documented the worry grows. For instance, disposing of liquid wastes deep within the earth and the filling of large dams have created man-made earthquakes in areas where previously there had been no seismic activity. The danger is that the artificial earthquakes, which have destroyed life and property, may trigger a mighty one that could wipe out a heavily populated area.

Dust, smoke, and other particles put into the air from bad farming practices, factories, and other sources of pollution are cutting off the warming rays of the sun, and many scientists believe that is the reason that the earth's temperature has dropped since 1940. The danger: man may be setting the stage for a new ice age.

High-flying jets have already caused an estimated 5

to 10 percent increase in the cirrus cloud cover over the areas of their regular routes. The supersonic aircraft will do even more, possibly creating a total cloud covering over their paths.

As the clouds increase, the warmth of the sun (the earth's basic source of energy for living things) will decrease. Consequently, the earth will become cooler still. The trade winds exist because they are nature's way of balancing the great heat input at the equator with the rest of the planet. With less heat reaching the ground, there will be less energy to push the winds. As the warm air reaching the poles decreases, the poles will become colder and the ice fields will grow. That may be another factor leading to a new ice age.

Your ability to take a good, long breath of air may be seriously hampered, even if you live in the country. Threatened chemical poisoning of the oceans, where more than half of the earth's oxygen supply comes from, may require people to wear oxygen masks just as they would if they visited Mars or another desolate planet.

The pesticides and fertilizers that reach us through our food chain affect all living creatures on land, in the air, and even deep in the sea. They pose another hazard to our environment, creating a biological time bomb that is already ticking. . . .

Never before has man had the means or the ability to rival nature's power to alter the world. When the Greek mathematician and inventor, Archimedes, said centuries ago that if he had a long enough lever and a place to stand he could move the earth he knew that no such lever existed.

Modern man, however, has stumbled across some of Archimedes' "levers." In the dash for profit and comfort, man has used his impressive science and technology to make wholesale changes without thinking them through to find out what effect they will have on his spaceship, earth.

He produced the automobiles that envelop our cities in smog long before anyone understood the harmful effects of exhausts on health. He made insecticides before anyone learned that they also kill animals and might be harmful to people. He produced synthetic detergents and put billions of pounds into the rivers and lakes before he realized that he couldn't get rid of them. Instead they polluted our waterways and caused them to age prematurely—Lake Erie has become America's "dead sea." And he spread radioactive fallout across the globe from nuclear bomb tests before he discovered that the danger to living things was too great to let it continue. . . .

Man's misuse of his environment is not new. In the past, however, it was generally limited to local areas. When one region became despoiled, man could always move across the hill to greener pastures. He no longer has this luxury.

The great Babylonian empire vanished when the farmlands that made it thrive could no longer grow crops. Inadequate agricultural practices allowed fertility-destroying salts to accumulate in the soil. Ancient Greece once had forested hills. When the trees were cut down, the soil eroded and the springs dried up. Other civilizations have perished because of unexpected changes in their environment. . . .

Nature offers no blank check for the amount of abuse she will take. There is a limit. Our atmosphere is held to the earth by the pull of gravity. It is a living atmosphere, continuously being used and renewed. Its existence depends on a complex but delicate balance that took nature billions of years to reach. There was no oxygen on our primeval planet—nature squeezed it out, molecule by molecule, until, through evolution, she built up a plant system using photosynthesis, a process that manufactures enough oxygen to keep humans alive.

But life on earth is only skin deep. Though you can travel around the world and find living things in most places, if you go more than two miles up in the atmosphere, you will find practically nothing. If you go more than a half mile down in the oceans, you will again just about run out of living things to see. The thin wafer between these two limits is the biosphere, and it contains our life-support system that enables us to ride on our spaceship.

But enormous waste products from man's activities have been dumped into the atmosphere, the oceans, and even into the solid earth, creating a mad scramble in nature to readjust. Man is putting stresses on nature in ways that could cause her to snap back angrily.

One of her angry responses is evident in the earth's changing climate, possibly heading us toward a cold world, according to Dr. Reid A. Bryson, a University of Wisconsin climatologist. The rapid increase in dust and smoke pollution is perhaps the primary cause for nearly half a degree drop in the earth's average temperature since 1940, he says. The particulate pollution acts like an umbrella that blocks the sun's visible energy from reaching the earth.

Although a half a degree doesn't sound like much, a drop of only 7.2 to 9 degrees could start the advance of a new ice age. With the fall in temperature already recorded, the frost and ice boundaries have begun creeping south. They were accompanied by weakening air circulation and marked increases in rainfall in parts of the previously arid continental areas. Last year the sea ice coverage in the North Atlantic was the most extensive in over 60 years; Icelandic fishermen suffered great losses while the increased rains in the central continental regions, particularly India, led to very high wheat yields.

"It appears that population growth, mechanization, and industrialization have now made man the equivalent of other natural processes in his effect on climate," Dr. Bryson says.

Prior to 1940, the earth had been getting warmer. Scientists believe this warming trend, like the current cooling trend, was also due to man-made pollution. The burning of increasing amounts of fossil fuels had spewed millions of tons of carbon dioxide into the air. Carbon dioxide climbed from 290 parts per million of air to 330 since the beginning of the century.

The waste gas from combustion creates a hothouse effect. It lets the sun's visible energy hit the earth but it reduces the amount of energy escaping from the earth. Normally part of the sun's radiation bounces back from the surface into space in the form of infrared rays. Carbon dioxide slows down the escape of these rays, consequently adding to the surface heat.

But the gigantic increase in dust, smoke, soot, and other particulate matter (tiny, solid particles that can float in the air) from agricultural and urban pollution has overwhelmed the warming effect and has reversed the temperature trend, Dr. Bryson suggests. There are millions of square miles of land shrouded by a dust cover, and winds carry the polluted air around the world.

"If we are right in assuming that the dust and smoke are the major cause of the temperature drop, then at the present rate there could be a significant growth of the ice caps in about 200 years," said Wayne M. Wendland, a climatologist on the Wisconsin campus.

The tiny particles of pollution also have another effect. They serve as condensation nuclei around which minute droplets of water can form and grow into raindrops, fog, hail, clouds, and thunderstorms.

The low clouds that tend to be formed from pollution particles are extremely dangerous to our environment. They are the earth's most effective shield in blocking the sun's rays, thereby rapidly reducing the heat on the surface. The world now averages a 31 percent coverage from clouds. Increasing this by just 5 percent would drop the temperature about 7.2 degrees, a drop close to that required for a return to an ice age. . . .

Another factor that may be adding to the world's cooling trend is man's increasing ability to turn the earth into a "mirror" that reflects the sun's rays. Sprawling cities and suburban areas and the proliferation of highways and farming increase the earth's reflective power. More of the sun's warmth is being reflected back into space.

Some of the energy that was formerly absorbed by the trees and plants that were sacrificed for progress is now being lost from the earth. An estimated million acres of land are being converted to paving, building, and other uses each year.

Turning from man the rain and cloudmaker to man the earthshaker reveals another new chapter in man's awesome ability to inadvertently change the world.

To think that man can cause an earthquake is like believing an ant can move Boulder Dam. But man has stumbled upon another "lever," a weak point in nature. The earth's crust has changed considerably over geologic time. These changes stretched and twisted the crust to build up pressure points, or what geologists call tectonic forces. When the pressure points slip, they cause an earthquake.

The filling of big dams or the pumping of liquid wastes into deep wells can trigger these pressure points to slip a notch or two. Like the doctor who knows exactly where to tap your knee to produce a reflex action in your leg, man has uncovered a way to nudge the earth's pent-up muscles. Results: reflex—on a grand scale.

The artificially produced earthquake can kill people and destroy property. The last one occurred on December 10, 1967, when a severe tremor shook the area around the Kogna Dam in India. It killed 200 persons in a nearby town and its damaging effects were felt throughout India.

The first indication that the creation of artificial lakes can cause earth tremors was discovered in 1945 after a detailed study of the records of Lake Mead, near Las Vegas, Nevada. No seismic activity had been recorded for the area for 15 years before the dam was completed. Lake Mead was formed by damming of the Colorado River by Boulder Dam.

Water started filling the dam in 1936. About a year later when the level had reached 328 feet, the first small earthquake was felt in the vicinity. Approximately 100 small tremors were felt in 1937 as the water continued to fill the dam. With the installation of seismographs in 1938, thousands of earthquakes were detected. The water reached its normal level of 525 feet in 1939, the same year that the biggest tremor was felt in the area.

The explanation for the artificially produced Lake Mead earthquakes is that the weight of the water, amounting to 35 billion tons, reactivated ancient faults in the area. However, the tremors were not just a simple readjustment of the crust to the water load since the energy released by the earthquakes far exceeded the pressure of the lake on the crust.

Somehow the weight of the lake triggered the release of tectonic forces that had been bound up for aeons like knotted muscles.

Another example of the dam-earthquake effect was observed in 1962, two years after the world's largest artificial lake began filling in Africa. The Kariba Dam was completed in 1960. It blocks the Zambezi River which runs along the border of Rhodesia and Zambia, another quake-free zone. As the water level rose, seismic activity increased, reaching a peak in September, 1963, with a magnitude of 6.1 on the Richter scale. Such an earthquake in an urban area could cause substantial damage.

"The man-made disturbances are approaching the critical magnitude range and there is not insignificant probability that a man-made event could set off a catastrophic earthquake," cautions Dr. Gordon F. MacDonald, Vice-Chancellor of the University of California at Santa Barbara.

San Francisco's 1906 earthquake caused damage totaling 250 to 300 million dollars. San Francisco lies in an active fault region and a similar earthquake today could produce losses reaching several billion dollars, MacDonald says.

Another area in which man is playing Russian roulette with nature is the threat that we may run out of oxygen. Already some heavily populated and industrialized countries use up more oxygen than they produce. The oceans, which produce 50 to 70 percent of the world's supply of oxygen, are being invaded by chemicals that could destroy their oxygen-producing capacity, a disaster that should cause us to catch our breath.

Dr. LaMont C. Cole, president of the American Institute of Biological Sciences, has sounded the warning bell about this hazard. Calculating the amount of oxygen needed for the combustion of fossil fuels in the contiguous United States for 1966 and balancing this with the amount of oxygen produced by photosynthesis in the country, Dr. Cole found that we are using 40 percent more oxygen than the land is producing.

"The implication is clear: We are absolutely dependent on oxygen which is produced outside our borders—mostly in the Pacific Ocean—and brought in by atmospheric circulation. If we should inadvertently kill enough marine diatoms or the organisms they depend on for fixed nitrogen, we would start running out of oxygen to breathe."

The life-saving diatom in the ocean that replenishes our oxygen supply is a tiny single-celled plant. There are zillions of these plants suspended in the water. Like their land-bound cousins, they produce oxygen through the process of photosynthesis.

What, asks Dr. Cole, would happen if a few tankers loaded with herbicides (powerful plant killers) sink in the Pacific—just as the oil tanker *Torrey Canyon* sank in the North Atlantic? Would this stop photosynthesis in the Pacific? A few such shipwrecks occurring close enough together in time might cause ultimate disaster!

The diatoms, however, are already under a life-threatening attack. DDT dust, which can suppress photosynthesis in water-borne plants, has been found far out at sea. Ocean birds, such as the Bermuda petrel, have been found to have high concentrations of the pesticide in their eggs. The chemical has had a damaging effect on their ability to reproduce.

The petrel is at the peak of the ocean food pyramid, and consequently gets substantial concentrations of DDT. The birds eat fish which eat diatoms, which, in turn, apparently gather DDT from the dust settling in the ocean.

"The growing spread of pollution has already shown up indirectly in midocean areas," says Dr. Francis S. Johnson, director of the earth and planetary sciences laboratory for the Southwest Center for Advanced Studies in Dallas.

"The sensitivity of phytoplankton (the ocean plant family of which diatoms are a member) to such materials is probably variable, and one cannot immediately discount the possibility that insecticide and herbicide pollution may have widespread and unforeseen effects that could affect the plankton that converts a large proportion of our carbon dioxide to oxygen," he adds.

Hundreds of other compounds are entering the oceans and little is known about their potential effects on marine life. Lead, for example, the anti-knock agent in gasoline, has even been found in increasing amounts at the North Pole. Like DDT, lead settles on all parts of the world, far from where it originated.

The *Torrey Canyon* incident, where 100,000 tons of crude oil were dumped on the ocean surface, is an instance where man attempted to correct a hazard, but not knowing the full effects of what he was doing, did greater damage.

According to Dr. J. Eric Smith, an English biologist who studied the 1967 disaster, the oil was relatively harmless to marine life and would have been naturally cleaned up in due time. Some of the mollusks, for example, were already beginning to eat the oil.

But, because the vast oil slick was a nuisance and threatened the economy of English coastal resorts, more than 3 million gallons of highly toxic detergents were poured over the beaches and open sea in an attempt to disperse the oil. The detergents were not harmless—they killed millions of fish and other forms of life.

"In the exposed middle reaches of the shore (where the detergents were sprayed) there developed within hours a scene of progressive devastation, and within a few days virtually nothing remained save for tufts of dead and dying algae. The rock surfaces were utterly bare of animals and littered at their bases with cemeteries of shells," reports Dr. Smith.

The huge 800-square-mile oil slick caused by the leak of Union Oil Company's undersea well off Santa Barbara, California, is another dramatic example of how man can unintentionally endanger his environment. It may take years or even a generation for the oil-soaked coastline to recover.

The oil pollution disaster could have "far-reaching ecological consequences which no one can predict," report zoologists Richard V. Bovbjerg and Hugh Dingle of the University of Iowa. The oil could destroy much of the food base for the California fishing industry in addition to killing large numbers of fish directly, they claim.

But a more ominous ocean oil pollution hazard is evolving, one which the National Academy of Sciences began worrying about in 1966. The oily coating over a large part of the ocean surfaces from accidents and discharges from ships may imperil the ocean's great energy engine—the transport of heat from the water to the atmosphere and vice-versa. Such an oily lid could seriously interfere with the earth's weather. . . .

The problems of pollution and unanticipated environmental hazards are increasing with an intensity that is directly proportional to the population explosion, AIBS's Dr. Cole says. Last summer the human population of the world passed 3.5 billion. At the present rate it is expected to double every 35 years.

"There is no possibility that the earth's environment can long sustain such pressure; in fact, I consider it very improbable that the earth could continually support, on a nondestructive basis, a population as large as the present one," he says.

"We shall have to decide, and soon, what quality of

life we want for ourselves and what steps in pollution and population control are necessary to get it." [6]

*If man possesses the power to end the world, does he have the power to save it? Can he avoid being his own doomsday machine? How?*

[6] Ronald Kotulak, "Is Man His Own Doomsday Machine?" *Chicago Tribune Magazine,* March 30, 1969, pp. 19-24. Reprinted courtesy of the *Chicago Tribune.*

## Bottom of the Ninth

NATURE BATS LAST!

## Unless We Guard Them Well

Perhaps the children of a future day
Between picnics on Venus and the moon
And explorations of the Milky Way
Will come and spend a summer afternoon
Among the quaint old-fashioned people, asking,
"And did you really see a robin, sir?
And even a clover field with cattle basking?
And could you tell us just what daisies were?"
Let us speak carefully of the long ago
Lost days when earth was green, and country air
Was filled with winging song and petaled glow
Lest any yearning listener may declare,
"Oh, I would give the moon if I had heard
A thrush, or ever seen a hummingbird!" [7]

## The Cancer Called Man

*"The problem of self-limitation of growth was solved a long time ago by cells; it had to be before the higher organism could develop. . . . All uncontrolled growths kill the host on which they live."* [8]

The first mistake is to think of mankind as a thing in itself.

It isn't.

It is part of an intricate web of life. And we can't think even of life as a thing in itself. It isn't. It is part of the

[7] Jane Merchant, *Because It's Here* (Nashville, Abingdon Press, 1970), p. 120. Copyright © 1970 by Abingdon Press.

[8] Robert Rienow and Leona Train Rienow, *Moment in the Sun* (New York: Ballantine Books, 1967, p. 15.

intricate structure of a planet bathed by energy from a sun.

The Earth, in the nearly five billion years since it assumed its present form, has undergone a vast evolution.

When it first came into being, it very likely lacked what we would today call an ocean and an atmosphere. These were formed by the gradual outward movement of material as the solid interior settled together.

Nor were ocean, atmosphere and solid crust independent of each other after formation. There is interaction always: evaporation, condensation, solution, weathering. Far within the solid crust there are slow continuing changes, too, of which hot springs, volcanoes and earthquakes are the more noticeable manifestations here on the surface.

Between two and three billion years ago, portions of the surface water, bathed by the energetic radiation from the sun, developed complicated compounds in organization sufficiently versatile to qualify as what we call "life."

Life-forms have become more complex and more various ever since.

But the life-forms are as much part of the structure of the Earth as any inanimate portion is. It is all an inseparable part of a whole.

If any animal is isolated totally from other forms of life, then death by starvation will surely follow. If isolated from water, death by dehydration will follow even faster. If isolated from air, whether free or dissolved in water, death by asphyxiation will follow still faster. If isolated from the sun, animals would survive for a time, but plants would die, and if all plants died, all animals would starve.

It works in reverse, too, for the inanimate portion of Earth is shaped and molded by life. The nature of the atmosphere has been changed by plant activity (which adds to the air the free oxygen it could not otherwise retain). The soil is turned by earthworms, while enormous ocean reefs are formed by coral.

The entire planet, plus solar energy, is one enormous intricately interrelated system. The entire planet is a life-form made up of non-living portions and a large variety of living portions (as our own body is made up of non-living crystals in bones and non-living water in blood, as well as of a large variety of living portions).

In fact, we can pursue the analogy. A man is composed of 50 trillion cells of a variety of types, all interrelated and interdependent. Loss of some of those cells, such as those making up an entire leg, will seriously handicap all the rest of the organism; serious damage to a relatively few cells in an organ such as the heart or kidneys may end by killing all 50 trillion.

In the same way, on a planetary scale, the chopping down of an entire forest may not threaten Earth's life in general, but it will produce serious changes in the life-forms of the region and even in the nature of the water run-off and, therefore, in the details of geological structure.

A serious decline in the bee population will affect the numbers of those plants that depend on bees for fertilization, then the numbers of those animals that depend on those particular bee-fertilized plants, and so on.

Or consider cell growth. Cells in those organs that suffer constant wear and tear—as in the skin or in the intestinal lining—grow and multiply all life long. Other cells not so exposed, as in nerve and muscle, do not multiply at all in the adult under any circumstances. Still other organs, ordinarily quiescent, as liver and bone, stand ready to grow if necessary to replace damage. When the proper repairs are made, growth stops.

In a much looser and more flexible way, the same is true of the "planet-organism" (which we study in the science called ecology). If cougars grow too numerous, the deer they live on are decimated and some of the cougars die of starvation so that their "proper number" is restored. If too many cougars die, then the deer multiply with particular rapidity and cougars multiply quickly in turn, till the additional predators bring down the number of deer again.

Barring interference from outside, the eaters and the eaten retain their proper numbers and both are the better for it. (If the cougars were all killed off, deer would multiply to the point where they destroy the plants they live off of, and more would then die of starvation than would have died of cougars.)

The neat economy of growth within an organism such as a human being is sometimes—for what reason, we know not—disrupted and a group of cells begins growing without limit. This is the dread disease of cancer and unless that growing group of cells is somehow stopped, the wild growth will throw all the body structure out of true, and end by killing the organism itself.

In ecology, the same would happen, if, for some reason, one particular type of organism began to multiply without limit, killing its own competitors and increasing its own food supply at the expense of that of others. That, too, could end only in the destruction of the larger system—most or all of life and even of certain aspects of the inanimate environment.

And this is exactly what is happening at this moment.

For thousands of years, the single species, *Homo sapiens,* to which you and I have the dubious honor of belonging, has been increasing in numbers. In the last couple of centuries, the rate of increase has itself increased explosively. At the time of Julius Caesar, when

Earth's human population is estimated to have been 150 million, that population was increasing at a rate such that it would double in a thousand years if that rate remained steady. Today, with Earth's population estimated at 3 billion 680 million (25 times what it was in Caesar's time) it is increasing at a rate which, if steady, will cause it to double in 35 years.

The present rate of increase of Earth's swarming human population qualifies *Homo sapiens* as an ecological cancer that will destroy the ecology just as surely as any ordinary cancer would destroy an organism.

The cure? Just what it is for any cancer. The cancerous growth must somehow be stopped.

Of course, it will be. If we do nothing at all, the growth will stop, as a cancerous growth in man will stop if nothing is done. The man dies and the cancer dies with him. And, analogously, the ecology will die and man will die with it.

How can the human population explosion be stopped? By raising the death rate, or by lowering the birth rate. There are no other alternatives. The death rate will rise spontaneously and finally catastrophically if we do nothing—and that within a few decades.

To make the birth rate fall somehow (almost *any* how, in fact) is surely preferable, and that is therefore the first order of mankind's business today.

Failing this, mankind would stand at the bar of abstract justice (for there may be no posterity to judge) as the mass murderer of life generally, his own included, and mass disrupter of the intricate planetary development that made life in its present glory possible in the first place.

Am I too pessimistic? Can we allow the present rate of population-increase to continue indefinitely, or at least for a good long time?

Can we count on science to develop methods for cleaning up as we pollute, for replacing wasted resources with substitutes, for finding new food, new materials, more and better life for our waxing numbers?

Impossible!—if the numbers continue to wax at the present rate.

Let us begin with a few estimates (admittedly not precise, but in the rough neighborhood of truth).

The total mass of living objects on Earth is perhaps 20 trillion tons.

There is usually a balance between eaters and eaten that is about 1 to 10 in favor of eaten. There would therefore be about ten times as much plant life (the eaten) as animal life (the eaters) on Earth. There is, in other words, just a little under 2 trillion tons of animal life on Earth.

But this is all the animal life that can exist, given the present quantity of plant life. If more animal life is somehow produced, it will strip down the plant life, reduce the food supply, and then enough animals will starve to restore the balance. If one species of animal life increases in mass, it can only be because other species correspondingly decrease.

For every additional pound of human flesh on Earth, a pound of some other form of flesh must disappear.

The total mass of humanity now on Earth may be estimated at about 200 million tons, or one-ten-thousandth the mass of all animal life. If mankind increases in numbers of 10,000-fold, then *Homo sapiens* will be, perforce, the only animal species alive on Earth.

It will be a world without elephants or lions, without cats or dogs, without fish or lobsters, without worms or bugs. What's more, to support the mass of human life, all the plant world must be put to service.

Only plants edible to man must remain; and only

those plants most concentratedly edible and with minimum of waste.

At the present moment, the average density of population of the Earth's land surface is about 73 people per square mile. Increase that 10,000-fold and the average density will become 730,000 people per square mile or more than seven times the density of the workday population of Manhattan.

Even if we assume that mankind will somehow spread itself into vast cities floating on the ocean surface (or resting on the ocean floor) the average density of human life at the time when the last non-human animal must be killed would be 310,000 people per square mile over all the world, land and sea alike, or a little better than three times the density of modern Manhattan at noon.

We have the vision, then, of high-rise apartments, higher and more thickly spaced than in Manhattan at present, spreading all over the world, across all the mountains, across the Sahara Desert, across Antarctica, across all the oceans; all with their load of humanity and with no other form of animal life. And on the roof of all those buildings are the algae farms, with little plant cells exposed to the sun so that they may grow rapidly and, without waste, form protein for all the mighty population of 35 trillion human beings.

Is that tolerable? Even if science produced all the energy and materials mankind could want, is the planetary high-rise tolerable?

And if it were, can we double the population further in 35 more years? And then double it again in another 35? Where will the food come from? What will persuade the algae to multiply faster than the light energy they absorb makes possible? What will speed up the sun to add the energy to make it possible?

And if vast supplies of fusion energy are added to supplement the sun, how will we get rid of the equally vast supplies of heat that will be produced? And after the ice caps are melted and the oceans boiled into steam, what?

Can we bleed off the mass of humanity to other worlds? Right now, the number of human beings on Earth is increasing by 100 million per year, and each year that number goes up by one and a fraction percent. Can we really suppose that we can send 100 million people per year to the moon, Mars, and elsewhere and engineer those worlds to support those people? And even so, merely remain in the same place ourselves?

No! Not the most optimistic visionary in the world could honestly convince himself that space-travel is the solution to our population problem, if the present rate of increase is sustained.

But when will this planetary high-rise culture come about? How long will it take to increase Earth's population to that impossible point at the present doubling rate of once every 35 years? If it will take a million years or even a hundred thousand then, for goodness sake, let's not worry just yet.

Well, we don't have that kind of time. We will reach that dead end in no more than 460 years.

At the rate we are going, without birth control, then even if science serves us in an absolutely ideal way, we will reach the planetary high-rise with no animals but man, with no plants but algae, with no room for even one more person, by A.D. 2430.

And if science serves us in less than an ideal way (as it certainly will) the end will come sooner, much sooner, and mankind will start fading long, long before he is forced to construct that building that will cover all the Earth's surface.

So, if birth control *must* come by A.D. 2430 at the

very latest, even in an ideal world of advancing science, let it come *now* in Heaven's name, while there are still oak trees in the world and daisies and tigers and butterflies, and while there is still open land and space, and before the cancer called Man proves fatal to life and the planet.[9]

*Popullution Simulation*

*Blindfold a friend or member of your study group, take him to a small room, and direct him with only verbal instructions to touch four widely separated objects in the room (doorknob, window ledge, chair, bookcase, lamps, etc.). Then each of you bring in another blindfolded person, and individually (and simultaneously) guide them, again by verbal instructions only, to perform the same task. Then all four of you each bring in another blindfolded person, individually and simultaneously guiding them, as before, to perform the same task. Then all eight of you each bring in a blindfolded person, etc.*

*Now, how do you feel about unrestricted population growth?*

[9] Isaac Asimov, "The Cancer Called Man," *Midwest Magazine*, June 14, 1970, pp. 34-37. Copyright 1970 by Field Enterprises Inc. Courtesy of Publishers-Hall Syndicate.

# At-One-Ment: Getting with Spaceship Earth

On the eve of the fifth day, when he saw that his Creation was good, God asked "And how am I, who am all-knowingly at one with my own Creation, to experience the wonder of its depths?" And so on the sixth day, upon completing the beginning of his Creation, God embodied himself in a form which enabled him to receive, enjoy, and care for the gift he had given. And this, too, was good.

*"If I had to choose, I would rather have birds than airplanes."*

*—Charles A. Lindbergh*

## Bank Accounts

Imagine that when you were born you were granted a bank account. Imagine further that this bank account contained all the money you would ever have. Once the money ran out, you would be absolutely unable to gain more from any other source. Imagine, finally, that the amount of money in your account was unknown. You would always know how much you have spent, but you would never know how much was left.

How would you spend your money?

* * * *

Did it ever occur to you that when you were born, you were granted a *life* account? This life account consists of all the days you have to live. Once these days run out, you will be unable to gain more of them. You do not know how many days you have to live. You can always compute how many days of your life have been spent, but you never know how many are left.

How do you spend your life?

* * * *

Did it ever occur to you that part of your life account consists of your environment? You were born on a planet which has finite material resources with which to sustain life. If these resources are ever depleted, you will be unable to gain more of them. With considerable difficulty we might be able to compute how much of the planet's life-sustaining resources have been consumed. But we do not know for how long the remaining resources of the planet will sustain, at the current standard of living, present (to say nothing of projected) population levels.

How do you spend your environment?

## Magic Mirrors

*"For with the judgment you pronounce you will be judged."* (*Matthew 7:2*)

Suppose that you have a magic mirror. This mirror does not reflect your external appearance, like other mirrors. It reflects your *internal* appearance. By looking in it you can see the state of your inner being. You can see not what you *look* like but what you *are* like.

The fact is, you have at least two such mirrors. One of them is the people around you. Consider Carl Sandburg's account of the Kansas sodbuster:

> *Who was that early sodbuster in Kansas? He leaned at the gatepost and studied the horizon and figured what corn might do next year and tried to calculate why God ever made the grasshopper and why two days of hot winds smother the life out of a stand of wheat and why there was such a spread between what he got for grain and the price quoted in Chicago and New York. Drove up a newcomer in a covered wagon: "What kind of folks live around here?" "Well, stranger, what kind of folks was there in the country you come from?" "Well, they was mostly a low-down, lying, thieving, gossiping, backbiting lot of people." "Well, I guess, stranger, that's about the kind of folks you'll find around here." And the dusty gray stranger had just about blended into the dusty gray cottonwoods in a clump on the horizon when another newcomer drove up: "What kind of folks live around here?" "Well, stranger, what kind of folks was there in the country you come from?" "Well, they was mostly a decent, hard-working, lawabiding, friendly lot of people." "Well, I guess, stranger, that's about*

*the kind of folks you'll find around here." And the second wagon moved off and blended with the dusty gray cottonwoods on the horizon while the early sod-buster leaned at his gatepost and tried to figure why two days of hot winds smother the life out of a nice stand of wheat.*[1]

How do you really feel about people in general, and about your friends and associates in particular? However you feel about them, whatever you decide about them, you are actually making a statement about who *you* are. Perhaps this is why people tend to form their feelings and decisions about you on the basis of what you say about others.

There is nothing which identifies who you *are* more quickly than those things which you find significant to openly consider in others. If you constantly remark upon the faults of others, people will know that you feel the need to divert attention from your own faults. If you find the good in others, people will recognize the goodness in yourself that makes possible your recognition of goodness elsewhere.

Your associates can see who you are by listening to what you say about other people. Can you?

*"For whatever a man sows, that he will also reap."*
*(Galatians 6:7)*

Your other magic mirror is the world about you. The environment also provides feedback concerning your inner state of being. Look at it (and listen to the quakings from underneath):

[1] Carl Sandburg, *The People, Yes* (New York: Harcourt, Brace & Co., 1936), p. 120.

The junk on its landscape reflects your obsession with material objects.

The sewage in its rivers reflects your contempt for material sustenance.

The filth in its air reflects your blindness to your own needs.

The garbage in its oceans reflects your rejection of the ground of your own being.

The rumblings in its bowels . . .

ARE YOU LISTENING?

## Something Is Right with the Earth

*"The universe is so successful, I simply want to learn its principles and apply them rather than to exploit it blindly and fear for survival."—R. Buckminster Fuller*

An interesting exercise is to write down the design criteria for a spaceship to carry a crew of 250 on a 40-year journey through space. Such criteria would include adequate radiation shielding; energy or fuel reserves required for instrument operation, navigation, and heating; assured supplies of air, water, and food for the crew throughout the journey; waste reprocessing and disposal; and many others. With such a list in hand, it is instructive to review the extent to which the earth considered as a spaceship fulfills each of the design criteria. One discovers in carrying out this exercise that the earth is amazingly well designed as a spaceship for carrying a crew of some two to three billion human beings, but not many more, on a long journey through space.

It would not be possible to design a more effective radiation shield for a spaceship than the earth's atmosphere. Although transparent to light it cuts out completely all the far ultraviolet, X rays, and higher-energy radiations of outer space. The aurora borealis magnificently displays this shield in operation as it keeps all the high-energy electrons and protons which bombard the earth above 60 miles from its surface. Under this efficient shield the only radiation hazard to which we are exposed is sunburn from the near ultraviolet which does get through.

Let us now consider in greater detail some of the other fundamental requirements for a satisfactory spaceship. First, it must have an adequate source of energy to last throughout the trip. Next, it must have an adequate food supply or means of producing food for the crew. The air and water reserves in the ship must be kept pure and adequate for all needs. Wastes must be reprocessed or disposed of in ways which will not contaminate the ship. Finally, the crew must not be allowed to increase in numbers, and it must remain unified throughout the journey. Divisions into warring rival subcrews or interpersonal conflicts between crew members would be catastrophic in a spaceship on an extended voyage.[2]

*Continue to develop, preferably as a group, the criteria required for a successful extended journey through space.*

## Something Is Right with You

Do something silly for a moment. Toss a precious object into the air and catch it. Now consider the ex-

[2] William G. Pollard, "The Earth as a Spaceship," *The Science Teacher*, September, 1969, p. 26.

traordinary device (you, yourself) that just accomplished this everyday miracle. You sensed the energy of the toss, knew the value and importance of success. You triangulated the position of the object throughout its flight with your binocular vision, you edited out distractions by other senses that might divert your attention, you brought an extraordinary signal mechanism into precise operation that triggered one set of muscles after another into a sequence of ground-to-air-missile direction-control processes resulting in easy success as you caught the object without thinking.

What you did will not make headlines anywhere. It is the simplest example I can think of of what you do millions of times a day. But ask your friends who know micro-electronics best what it would cost, and how much space it would take, to achieve artificially what you just achieved naturally. He will admit that the problem of reconstituting these simple excellences of yours would require a major federal grant. But that's just for the easy part.

Remember that all the miraculous abilities you demonstrated can be naturally and automatically packaged, and preserved without the slightest impairment, for periods of twenty to fifty years or so, in an ultramicroscopic part of you, received by you at no cost and forwarded into the future at the same price, in a tiny segment of a gene in a chromosome in a solution so concentrated that a single teaspoon could contain all the instructions needed to build and operate the three billion people now on the planet.[3]

[3] "Something Is Right With You," by David Brower, from Foreword to *Summer Island: Penobscot Country,* by Eliot Porter, copyright © 1966 by the Sierra Club. Reprinted by permission of the Sierra Club.

## . . . and It Was Very Good

You represent a fantastic investment. For four and a half billion years, billions upon billions of processes had to turn out a certain way for you to be here. Some of these processes were large ones, like the accumulation of the atmosphere. Some were small, like the direct chain of matings which stretches back from you to the origins of animal life. Your genes are the direct fruit of billions of conceptions, and the indirect fruit of trillions, all of which were successful. Something is right with the earth—you came out of it.

Your planet is indeed *Mother* Earth. It is perfectly equipped to raise and nurture you, as if it knew of your needs. But can you say the same in return?

Does it ever occur to you that the earth has needs? Do you know what they are?

Has it yet become apparent to you that you are as ideally equipped to nurture the planet as it is to nurture you?

Did you ever stop to realize that you are the means—and the only means—by which the earth can become *conscious* of its needs?

Is it beginning to dawn on you that only as the earth becomes fully conscious of its evolutionary possibilities can it achieve its potential in the Creation?

## Thinking the World Together

You didn't come into this world, any more than a blade of grass comes into this world. Like a blade of grass, you came *out of* this world. Trees bud. Flowers blossom. Earth peoples. So the world doesn't belong to you, you belong to it.

Take an inventory of what is right with your world. Find out what makes it right. And then *get with it*.

You have outgrown the luxury of being able to do things the wrong way. There are so many of us now that the sum total of our individual errors can spell inevitable disaster for all.

You can no longer do whatever you please *to* the earth. You must do what is necessary *with* the earth. Unless, that is, you are ready for the earth to do what is necessary with you.

To be with it, or not to be—that is the question.

## Powerhouse

*In the electric age we wear all mankind as our skin.*
*—Marshall McLuhan*

The horses moved gently to a stop, and the man and his wife gazed down into a dry, sandy valley. The woman sat lost in her saddle; she hadn't spoken for hours, didn't know a good word to speak. She was trapped somewhere between the hot, dark pressure of the storm-clouded Arizona sky and the hard, granite pressure of the wind-blasted mountains. A few drops of cool rain fell on her trembling hands.

She looked over at her husband wearily. He sat his dusty horse easily, with a firm quietness. She closed her eyes and thought of how she had been all of these mild years until today. She wanted to laugh at the mirror she was holding up to herself, but there was no way of doing even that; it would be somewhat insane. After all, it might just be the pushing of this dark weather, or the telegram they had taken from the messenger on horseback this morning, or the long journey now to town.

There was still an empty world to cross, and she was cold.

"I'm the lady who was never going to need religion," she said quietly, her eyes shut.

"What?" Berty, her husband, glanced over at her.

"Nothing," she whispered, shaking her head. In all the years, how *certain* she had been. Never, never would she have need of a church. She had heard fine people talk on and on of religion and waxed pews and calla lilies in great bronze buckets and vast bells of churches in which the preacher rang like a clapper. She had heard the shouting kind and the fervent, whispery kind, and they were all the same. Hers was simply not a pew-shaped spine.

"I just never had a reason ever to sit in a church," she had told people. She wasn't vehement about it. She just walked around and lived and moved her hands that were pebble-smooth and pebble-small. Work had polished the nails of those hands with a polish you could never buy in a bottle. The touching of children had made them soft, and the raising of children had made them temperately stern, and the loving of a husband had made them gentle.

And now, death made them tremble.

"Here," said her husband. And the horses dusted down the trail to where an odd brick building stood beside a dry wash. The building was all glazed green windows, blue machinery, red tile, and wires. The wires ran off on high-tension towers to the farthest directions of the desert. She watched them go, silently, and, still held by her thoughts, turned her gaze back to the strange storm-green windows and the burning-colored bricks.

She had never slipped a ribbon in a Bible at a certain significant verse, because though her life in this desert was a life of granite, sun, and the steaming away of the waters of her flesh, there had never been a threat to her.

Always things had worked out before the necessity had come for sleepless dawns and wrinkles in the forehead. Somehow, the very poisonous things of life had passed her. Death was a remote storm rumor beyond the farthest range.

Twenty years had blown in tumbleweeds, away, since she'd come west, worn this lonely trapping man's gold ring, and taken the desert as a third, and constant, partner to their living. None of their four children had ever been fearfully sick or near death. She had never had to get down on her knees except for the scrubbing of an already well-scrubbed floor.

Now all that was ended. Here they were riding toward a remote town because a simple piece of yellow paper had come and said very plainly that her mother was dying.

And she could not imagine it—no matter how she turned her head to see or turned her mind to look in on herself. There were no rungs anywhere to hold to, going either up or down, and her mind like a compass left out in a sudden storm of sand, was suddenly blown free of all its once-clear directions, all points of reference worn away, the needle spinning without purpose, around, around. Even with Berty's arms on her back it wasn't enough. It was like the end of a good play and the beginning of an evil one. Someone she loved was actually going to die. This was impossible!

"I've got to stop," she said, not trusting her voice at all, so she made it sound irritated to cover her fear.

Berty knew her as no irritated woman, so the irritation did not carry over and fill him up. He was a capped jug; the contents there for sure. Rain on the outside didn't stir the brew. He side-ran his horse to her and took her hand gently. "Sure," he said. He squinted at the eastern sky. "Some clouds piling up back there. We'll wait a bit. It might rain. I wouldn't want to get caught in it."

Now she was irritated at her own irritation, one fed upon the other, and she was helpless. But rather than speak and risk the cycle's commencing again, she slumped forward and began to sob, allowing her horse to be led until it stood and tramped its feet softly beside the red brick building.

She slid down like a parcel into his arms, and he held her as she turned in on his shoulder; then he set her down and said, "Don't look like there's people here." He called, "Hey, there!" and looked at the sign on the door: *Danger, Bureau of Electric Power.*

There was a great insect humming all through the air. It sang in a ceaseless, bumbling tone, rising a bit, perhaps falling just a bit, but keeping the same pitch. Like a woman humming between pressed lips as she makes a meal in the warm twilight over a hot stove. They could see no movement within the building; there was only the gigantic humming. It was the sort of noise you would expect from hot railroad ties on a blazing summer day, when there is that flurried silence and you see the air eddy and whorl and ribbon, and expect a sound from the process but get nothing but an arched tautness of the eardrums and the tense quiet.

The humming came up through her heels, into her medium-slim legs, and thence to her body. It moved to her heart and touched it, as the sight of Berty just sitting on a top rail of the corral often did. And then it moved on to her head and the slenderest niches in the skull and set up a singing, as love songs and good books had done once on a time.

The humming was everywhere. It was as much a part of the soil as the cactus. It was as much a part of the air as the heat.

"What is it?" she asked, vaguely perplexed, looking at the building.

"I don't know much about it except it's a powerhouse," said Berty. He tried the door. "It's open," he said, surprised. "I wish someone was around." The door swung wide and the pulsing hum came out like a breath of air over them, louder.

They entered together into the solemn, singing place. She held him tightly, arm in arm.

It was a dim undersea place, smooth and clean and polished, as if something or other was always coming through and coming through and nothing ever stayed, but always there was motion and motion, invisible and stirring and never settling. On each side of them as they advanced were what first appeared to be people standing quietly, one after the other, in a double line. But these resolved into round, shell-like machines from which the humming sprang. Each black and gray and green machine gave forth golden cables and lime-colored wires, and there were silver metal pouches with crimson tabs and white lettering, and a pit like a washtub in which something whirled as if rinsing unseen materials at invisible speeds. The centrifuge raced so fast it stood still. Immense snakes of copper looped down from the twilight ceiling, and vertical pipes webbed up from cement floor to fiery brick wall. And the whole of it was as clean as a bolt of green lightning and smelled similarly. There was a crackling, eating sound, a dry rustling as of paper; flickers of blue fire shuttled, snapped, sparked, hissed where wires joined porcelain bobbins and green glass insulation.

Outside, in the real world, it began to rain.

She didn't want to stay in this place; it was no place to stay, with its people that were not people but dim machines and its music like an organ caught and pressed on a low note and a high note. But the rain washed every window and Berty said, "Looks like it'll last. Might have to stay the night here. It's late, anyhow. I'd better get the stuff in."

She said nothing. She wanted to be getting on. Getting on to what thing in what place, there was really no way of knowing. But at least in town she would hold onto the money and buy the tickets and hold them tight in her hand and hold onto a train which would rush and make a great noise, and get off the train, and get another horse, or get into a car hundreds of miles away and ride again, and stand at last by her dead or alive mother. It all depended on time and breath. There were many places she would pass through, but none of them would offer a thing to her except ground for her feet, air for her nostrils, food for her numb mouth. And these were worse than nothing. Why go to her mother at all, say words, and make gestures? she wondered. What would be the use?

The floor was clean as a solid river under her. When she moved forward on it, it sent echoes cracking back and forth like small, faint, gunshots through the room. Any word that was spoken came back as from a granite cavern.

Behind her, she heard Berty setting down the equipment. He spread two gray blankets and put out a little collection of tinned foods.

It was night. The rain still streamed on the high green-glazed windows, rinsing and making patterns of silk that flowed and intermingled in soft clear curtains. There were occasional thunderclaps which fell and broke upon themselves in avalanches of cold rain and wind hitting sand and stone.

Her head lay upon a folded cloth, and no matter how she turned it, the humming of the immense powerhouse worked up through the cloth into her head. She shifted, shut her eyes, and adjusted herself, but it went on and on. She sat up, patted the cloth, lay back down.

But the humming was there.

She knew without looking, by some sense deep in herself, that her husband was awake. There was no year she could remember when she hadn't known. It was some subtle difference in his breathing. It was the absence of sound, rather; no sound of breathing at all, save at long carefully thought-out intervals. She knew that he was looking at her in the rainy darkness, concerned with her, taking great care of his breath.

She turned in the darkness. "Berty?"

"Yes?"

"I'm awake too," she said.

"I know," he said.

They lay, she very straight, very rigid, he in a half curl, like a hand relaxed, half bent inward. She traced this dark, easy curve and was filled with incomprehensible wonder.

"Berty," she asked, and paused a long while, "how . . . how are you like you are?"

He waited a moment. "How do you mean?" he said.

"How do you *rest?*" She stopped. It sounded very bad. It sounded so much like an accusation, but it was not, really. She knew him to be a man concerned with all things, a man who could see in darknesses and who was not conceited because of his ability. He was worried for her now, and for her mother's life or death, but he had a way of worrying that seemed indifferent and irresponsible. It was neither of the two. His concern was all in him, deep; but it lay side by side with some faith, some belief that accepted it, made it welcome, and did not fight it. Something in him took hold of the sorrow first, got acquainted with it, knew each of its traceries before passing the message on to all of his waiting body. His body held a faith like a maze, and the sorrow that struck into him was lost and gone before it finally reached where it wanted to hurt him. Sometimes this faith drove her into a senseless anger, from which she recovered quickly, knowing how useless it was to criticize something as contained as a stone in a peach.

"Why didn't I ever catch it from you?" she said at last.

He laughed a little bit, softly. "Catch what?"

"I caught everything else. You shook me up and down in other ways. I didn't know anything but what you taught me." She stopped. It was hard to explain. Their life had been like the warm blood in a person passing through tissues quietly, both ways.

"Everything but religion," she said. "I never caught that from you."

"It's not a catching thing," he said. "Someday you just relax. And there it is."

Relax, she thought. Relax what? The body. But how to relax the mind? Her fingers twitched beside her. Her eyes wandered idly about the vast interior of the powerhouse. The machines stood over her in dark silhouettes with little sparkles crawling on them. The humming-humming-humming crept along her limbs.

Sleepy. Tired. She drowsed. Her eyes lidded and opened and lidded and opened. The humming-humming-humming filled her marrow as if small hummingbirds were suspended in her body and in her head.

She traced the half-seen tubing up and up to the ceiling, and she saw the machines and heard the invisible whirlings. She suddenly became very alert in her drowsiness. Her eyes moved swiftly up and up and then down and across, and the humming-singing of the machines grew louder and louder, and her eyes moved, and her body relaxed; and on the tall, green windows she saw the shadows of the high-tension wires rushing off into the raining night.

Now the humming was in her, her eyes jerked, she felt herself yanked violently upright. She felt seized by a whirling dynamo, around, around in a whirl, out, out, into the heart of whirling invisibilities, fed into, accepted by a thousand copper wires, and shot, in an instant, over the earth!

She was everywhere at once!

Streaking along high monster towers in instants, sizzling between high poles where small glass knobs sat like crystal green birds holding the wires in their non-conductive beaks, branching in four directions, eight secondary directions, finding towns, hamlets, cities, racing on to farms, ranches, haciendas, she descended gently like a widely filamented spider web upon a thousand square miles of desert!

The earth was suddenly more than many separate things, more than houses, rocks, concrete roads, a horse here or there, a human in a shallow, boulder-topped grave, a prickling of cactus, a town invested with its own light surrounded by night, a million apart things. Suddenly it all had one pattern encompassed and held by the pulsing electric web.

She spilled out swiftly into rooms where life was rising from a slap on a naked child's back, into rooms where life was leaving bodies like the light fading from an electric bulb—the filament glowing, fading, finally colorless. She was in every town, every room, making light-patterns over hundreds of miles of land; seeing, hearing everything, not alone any more, but one of thousands of people, each with his ideas and his faiths.

Her body lay, a lifeless reed, pale and trembling. Her mind, in all its electric tensity, was flung about this way, that, down vast networks of powerhouse tributary.

Everything balanced. In one room she saw life wither; in another, a mile away, she saw wineglasses lifted to the newborn, cigars passed, smiles, handshakes, laughter. She saw the pale, drawn faces of people at white deathbeds, heard how they understood and accepted death, saw their gestures, felt their feelings, and saw that they, too, were lonely in themselves, with no way to get to the world to see the balance, see it as she was seeing it now.

She swallowed. Her eyelids flickered and her throat burned under her upraised fingers.

She was not alone.

The dynamo had whirled and flung her with centrifugal force out along a thousand lines into a million glass capsules screwed into ceilings, plucked into light by a pull of a cord or a twist of a knob or a flick of a switch.

The light could be in *any* room; all that was needed was to touch the switch. All rooms were dark until light came. And here she was, in all of them at once. And she was not alone. Her grief was but one part of a vast grief, her fear only one of countless others. And this grief was only a half thing. There was the other half; of things born, of comfort in the shape of a new child, of food in the warmed body, of colors for the eye and sounds in the awakened ear, and spring wild flowers for the smelling.

Whenever a light blinked out, life threw another switch; rooms were illuminated afresh.

She was with those named Clark and those named Gray and the Shaws and Martins and Hanfords, the Fentons, the Drakes, the Shattucks, the Hubbells, and the Smiths. Being alone was not alone, except in the mind. You had all sorts of peekholes in your head. A silly, strange way to put it, perhaps, but there were the holes; the ones to see through and see that the world was there and people in it, as hard put to and as uneasy as yourself; and there were the holes for hearing, and the one for speaking out your grief and getting rid of it, and the holes for knowing the changes of season through the scents of summer grain or winter ice or autumn fires. They were there to be used so that one was not alone. Loneliness was a shutting of the eyes. Faith was a simple opening.

The light-net fell upon all the world she had known for twenty years, herself blended with every line. She glowed and pulsed and was gentled in the great easy fabric. It lay across the land, covering each mile like a gentle, warm, and humming blanket. She was everywhere.

In the powerhouse the turbines whirled and hummed and the electric sparks, like little votive candles, jumped and clustered upon bent elbows of electric piping and glass. And the machines stood like saints and choruses, haloed now yellow, now red, now green, and a massed singing bent along the roof hollows and echoed down in endless hymns and chants. Outside the wind clamored at the brick walls and drenched the glazed windows with rain; inside, she lay upon her small pillow and suddenly began to cry.

Whether it was with understanding, acceptance, joy, resignation, she couldn't know. The singing went on, higher and higher, and she was everywhere. She put out her hand, caught hold of her husband, who was still awake, his eyes fixed at the ceiling. Perhaps he had run everywhere, too, in this instant, through the network of light and power. But then, he had always been everywhere at once. He felt himself a unit of a whole and therefore he was stable; to her, unity was new and shaking. She felt his arms suddenly around her and she pressed her face into his shoulder for a long while, hard, while the humming and the humming climbed higher, and she cried freely, achingly, against him. . . .

In the morning the desert sky was very clear. They walked from the powerhouse quietly, saddled their horses, cinched on all of the equipment, and mounted.

She settled herself and sat there under the blue sky. And slowly she was aware of her back, and her back was straight, and she looked at her alien hands on the reins, and they had ceased trembling. And she could see the far mountains; there was no blur nor a running-of-color to things. All was solid stone touching stone, and stone touching sand, and sand touching wild flower, and wild flower touching the sky in one continuous clear flow, everything definite and of a piece.

"Wope!" cried Berty, and the horses walked slowly off, away from the brick building, through the cool sweet morning air.

She rode handsomely and she rode well, and in her, like a stone in a peach, was a peacefulness. She called to her husband as they slowed on a rise, "Berty!"

"Yes?"

"Can we . . ." she asked.

"Can we what?" he said, not hearing the first time.

"Can we come here again sometime?" she asked, nodding back toward the powerhouse. "Once in a while? Some Sunday?"

He looked at her and nodded slowly. "I reckon. Yes. Sure. I reckon so."

And as they rode on into town she was humming, humming a strange soft tune, and he glanced over and listened to it, and it was the sound you would expect to hear from sun-warmed railroad ties on a hot summer day when the air rises in a shimmer, flurried and whorling; a sound in one key, one pitch, rising a little, falling a little, humming, humming, but constant, peaceful, and wondrous to hear.[4]

*"We are members one of another."—Ephesians 4:25*

*What are the practical implications of the statement, "In the electrical age we wear all mankind as our skin"? What are the spiritual implications? How does this story speak to the Christian concern with sin (feeling separated), conversion, and redemption? What does the powerhouse symbolize?*

## Put Yourself in the Planet's Shoe

*There was an old woman who lived in a shoe,*
*She had so many children she didn't know what to do.*
*She gave them some broth without any bread,*
*And whipped them all soundly and sent them to bed.*

Assume for a moment that the planet is intelligent, that it knows what it is doing, that it can analyze a problem, and that it can effect a solution.

Assume, then, that the planet knows, as we do, that every time an additional member is added to the United States population, the planet will eventually have to provide:

| | |
|---:|---|
| 56,000,000 | gallons of water |
| 21,000 | gallons of gasoline |
| 10,150 | lbs. of meat |
| 28,000 | lbs. of milk and ice cream |
| 9,000 | lbs. of wheat |
| 100,000 | lbs. of steel |
| 1,000 | trees |

[4] Ray Bradbury, "Powerhouse." Copyright 1952 by Ray Bradbury, reprinted by permission of the Harold Matson Company, Inc.

For each additional person in the United States, the planet will also have to provide space for 150,000 lbs. of garbage and cope with 140,000 lbs. of poison in its air.

Assume that the planet also knows, as we do, that the net increase of the United States population is approximately 3,759,500 a year. This means that each year the planet will eventually have to provide an additional

| | |
|---|---|
| 210,572,000,000,000 | gallons of water |
| 78,950,500,000 | gallons of gasoline |
| 38,118,325,000 | lbs. of meat |
| 105,266,000,000 | lbs. of milk and ice cream |
| 3,759,500,000,000 | lbs. of steel |
| 3,759,500,000 | trees |

to say nothing of providing space for 463,850,000,000 lbs. of garbage, and coping with 526,330,000,000 lbs. of poison in its air.

The problem is this:

1. The above figures are but a fraction of the total goods and services which will be required by the 3,759,500 persons born this year.
2. The planet will have a similar additional demand placed upon it each time another year goes by.
3. The planet still has to provide a proportionate annual share of goods and services for the 200,000,000 Americans already living (multiply the first set of figures by 200,000,000, and divide by the life expectancy of 70 years, to derive this proportionate annual share).
4. The planet must also provide goods and services for the other 93 percent of its human population, to say nothing of the demands placed upon it by its nonhuman population.
5. There is a limit to the planet's available goods and services.

The planet has only one available solution to choose: reduce its human population. However, it has several alternative methods for achieving such reduction:

1. On the basis of its past experience and its knowledge of present potentials, it can count on the strong possibility of man's solving the problem himself via nuclear warfare. This would be the easiest of all solutions, because it would establish a rapid equilibrium. The amount of life which would continue on the planet would be directly proportionate to the amount of resources which survived or avoided radioactive contamination.
2. The planet can fail to provide enough food. Again, man is providing a lot of assistance, especially in the United States, where approximately one acre of land is being removed from cultivation for each four persons added to the population.
3. The planet can let us die from our own poisons. Obviously, this solution is already being tried.
4. The planet can adopt earlier methods of population control—epidemic, the plague. Again, some experimentation with this method seems to be in progress.[5]

*What would you do if you were in the planet's shoe? You are, you know.*

*So what would you do? Give up?*

*That's a good place to start.* What *are you going to give up?*

[5] The statistics in this section are taken or computed from Robert Rienow and Leona Train Rienow, *Moment in the Sun;* literature from the National Congress on Optimum Population and Environment, 65 East Huron Street, Chicago, Illinois; and *U.S. News and World Report,* August 17, 1970, pp. 38-42.

# How I Got Radicalized: The Making of an Agitator for Zero

To my astonishment, the political convictions that I had cherished for most of my life have suddenly deserted me. Like my children, these were convictions I loved dearly and had nurtured at considerable expense. When last seen they were—like all of us—somewhat battered by the events of the last decade, but they looked durable enough to last out my time. So I was disconcerted when I found that somehow, during the past winter, they sort of melted away, without my consent and while I was looking somewhere else.

Their place has been usurped by a new set of convictions so radical that they alarm me. If the opposite kind of thing had happened, I would have felt a little melancholy but not surprised since people traditionally grow more conservative as they get older. But to discover that one has suddenly turned into a militant subversive is downright embarrassing; at times I wonder whether it signals the onset of second childhood.

Except that I seem to be a lot more radical than the children. Those SDS youngsters who go around breaking windows and clubbing policemen now merely depress me with their frivolous irrelevance. So do most other varieties of New Leftists, such as the Women's Liberation movement; if some dire accident should, God forbid, throw one of those ladies into my clutches, she can be sure of instant liberation. I am equally out of tune with those old fogies, the Communists. The differences between capitalism and Communism no longer seem to me worth fighting about, or even arguing, since they are both wrong and beside the point. Or so it seems to me, since the New Vision hit me on my own small road to Damascus.

Let me make it plain that none of this was my doing. I feel as Charles Darwin must have felt during the last leg of his voyage on the *Beagle*. When he embarked he had been a conventional (if slightly lackadaisical) Christian, who took the literal truth of Genesis for granted. He had been raised in that faith, as I was raised a Brass Collar Democrat, and had no thought of forsaking it. Only gradually, while he examined fossil shellfish high in the Andes and measured the growth of coral deposits and the bills of Galapagos finches, did he begin to doubt that the earth and all its inhabitants had been created in six days of October, 4004 B.C., according to the pious calculations of Archbishop James Ussher. By the time he got back to England, he found himself a reluctant evolutionist, soon to be damned as a heretic and underminer of the Established Church. This was not his fault. It was the fault of those damned finches.

Recently I too have been looking at finches, so to speak, although mine are mostly statistical and not nearly as pretty as Darwin's. His gave him a hint about the way the earth's creatures came into being; mine, to my terror, seem to hint at the way they may go out. While I am by no means an uncritical admirer of the human race, I have become rather fond of it, and would hate to see it disappear. Finding ways to save it—if we are not too late already—now strikes me as the political issue which takes precedence over all others.

One of the events which led to my conversion was my unexpected appointment to a committee set up by Governor John Dempsey of Connecticut to work out an environmental policy for our state. Now I had been fretting for quite a while about what is happening to our environment—who hasn't?—but until the work of the committee forced me into systematic study, I had not realized that my political convictions were in danger.

Then after looking at certain hairy facts for a few months, I found myself convinced that the Democratic party, and most of our institutions of government, and even the American Way of Life are no damned good. In their present forms, at least, they will have to go. Either that, or everybody goes—and sooner than we think.

To begin with, look at the American Way of Life. Its essence is a belief in growth. Every Chamber of Commerce is bent on making its Podunk grow into the Biggest Little City in the country. Wall Street is dedicated to its search for growth stocks, so that Xerox has become the American ideal—superseding George Washington, who expressed *his* faith in growth by speculating in land. Each year Detroit prays for a bigger car market. Businessmen spend their lives in pursuit of an annual increase in sales, assets, and net profits. All housewives—except for a few slatterns without ambition—yearn for bigger houses, bigger cars, and bigger salary checks. The one national goal that everybody agrees on is an ever-growing Gross National Product. Our modern priesthood—the economists who reassure us that our mystic impulses are moral and holy—recently announced that the GNP would reach a trillion dollars early this decade. I don't really understand what a trillion is, but when I read the news I rejoiced, along with everybody else. Surely that means that we were in sight of ending poverty, for the first time in human history, so that nobody would ever again need to go hungry or live in a slum.

Now I know better. In these past months I have come to understand that a zooming Gross National Product leads not to salvation, but to suicide. So does a continuing growth in population, highway mileage, kilowatts, plane travel, steel tonnage, or anything else you care to name.

The most important lesson of my life—learned shamefully late—was that non-stop growth just isn't possible, for Americans or anybody else. For we live in what I've learned to recognize as a tight ecological system: a smallish planet with a strictly limited supply of everything, including air, water, and places to dump sewage. There is no conceivable way in which it can be made bigger. If *Homo sapiens* insists on constant growth, within this system's inelastic walls, something has to pop, or smother. Already the United States is an overpopulated country: not so hopelessly overcrowded as Japan or India of course, but well beyond the limits which would make a good life attainable for everybody. Stewart Udall, former Secretary of Interior and now a practicing ecologist, has estimated that the optimum population for America would be about 100 million, or half our present numbers. And unless we do something, drastic and fast, we can expect another 100 million within the next thirty years.

So our prime national goal, I am now convinced, should be to reach Zero Growth Rate as soon as possible. Zero growth in people, in GNP, and in our consumption of everything. That is the only hope of attaining a stable ecology: that is, halting the deterioration of the environment on which our lives depend.

This of course is a profoundly subversive notion. It runs squarely against the grain of both capitalism and the American dream. It is equally subversive of Communism, since the Communists are just as hooked on the idea of perpetual growth as any American businessman. Indeed, when Khrushchev was top man in the Kremlin, he proclaimed that 1970 would be the year in which the Russians would surpass the United States in output of goods. They didn't make it: a fact for which their future generations may be grateful, because their environment is just as fragile as ours, and as easily damaged by headlong expansion. If you think the Hudson River and Lake Erie are unique examples of pollution, take a look at the Volga and Lake Baikal.

No political party, here or abroad, has yet even considered adopting Zero Growth Rate as the chief plank in its platform. Neither has any politician dared to speak out loud about what "protection of the environment" really means—although practically all of them seem to have realized, all of a sudden, that it is becoming an issue they can't ignore. So far, most of them have tried to handle it with gingerly platitudes, while keeping their eyes tightly closed to the implications of what they say. In his January State of the Union message, for instance, President Nixon made the customary noises about pollution; but he never mentioned the population explosion, and he specifically denied that there is any "fundamental contradiction between economic growth and the quality of life." He sounded about as convincing as a doctor telling a cancer patient not to worry about the growth of his tumor.

The Democrats are no better, I have not heard any of them demanding a halt to all immigration, or a steeply progressive income tax on each child beyond two, or an annual bounty to every woman between the ages of fifteen and forty-five who gets through the year without becoming pregnant. Neither Ted Sorensen nor any of the other Kennedy henchmen has yet suggested that a politician with a big family is a spacehog and a hypocrite, unworthy of public trust. No Democrat, to my knowledge, has ever endorsed the views of Dr. Rene Dubos of Rockefeller University, one of the truly wise men of our time. In an editorial in the November 14, 1969, issue of *Science* he predicted that in order to survive, "mankind will have to develop what might be called a steady state,

. . . a nearly closed system" in which most materials from tin cans to sewage would be "recycled instead of discarded." His conclusion—that a viable future depends on the creation of "social and economic systems different from the ones in which we live today"—apparently is too radical for any politician I know.

Consequently I feel a little lonesome in my newfound political convictions. The only organization which seems to share them is a tiny one, founded only a few months ago: Zero Population Growth, Inc., with headquarters at 367 State Street, Los Altos, California, 94022. Yet I have a hunch that I may not be lonesome for long. Among college students a concern with ecology has become, almost overnight, nearly as popular as sideburns. On many campuses it seems to be succeeding civil rights and Vietnam as The Movement. For example, when the University of Oregon announced last January a new course, "Can Man Survive?" it drew six thousand students, the biggest class in the university's history. They had to meet in the basketball court because no classroom would hold them.

Who knows? Maybe we agitators for Zero may yet turn out to be the wave of the future.[6]

*Are there forms of growth other than quantitative increase and accumulation? Can the economy, population, etc., like the human individual, continue to grow after stabilizing at a certain size?*

*Are there alternative solutions to the problem of living in a world with limited resources? Is it possible to rise above such limitation through a more effective application of technology?*

[6] John Fisher, "How I Got Radicalized: The Making of an Agitator for Zero," *Harper's Magazine*, April, 1970.

## Undertakings

At the same time I was losing my faith in the virtues of growth, I began to doubt two other articles of the American credo.

One of them is the belief that technology can fix anything. Like most of us, I had always taken it for granted that any problem could be solved if we just applied enough science, money, and good old American know-how. Is the world's population outrunning its food supply? Well, then, let's put the laboratories to work inventing high-yield strains of rice and wheat, better fertilizers, ways to harvest seaweed, hydroponic methods for growing food without soil. If the air is becoming unbreathable, surely the technologists can find ways to clean it up. If our transportation system is a national disgrace, all we have to do is call in the miracle men who built a shuttle service to the moon: certainly they should be able to figure out some way to get a train from New York to New Haven on time.

I was in East Haddam, Connecticut, looking at an atomic power plant, when I began to suspect that technology might not be the answer after all. While I can't go along with the young Luddites who have decided that science is evil and that all inventions since the wheel ought to be destroyed, I am persuaded that technology is a servant of only limited usefulness, and highly unreliable. When it does solve a problem, it often creates two new ones—and their side effects are usually hard to foresee.

One of the things that brought me to East Haddam was curiosity about the automobile. Since the gasoline engine is the main polluter of the air, maybe it should be replaced with some kind of electric motor? That of course would require an immense increase in our production of electric power, in order to recharge ten million batteries every night. Where would it come from? Virtually all waterpower sites already are in use. More coal and oil-fired power stations don't sound like a good idea, since they too pour smoke into the atmosphere—and coal mining already has ruined countless streams and hundreds of thousands of acres of irreplaceable land. Atomic power, then?

At first glance, the East Haddam plant, which is fairly typical of the new technology, looked encouraging. It is not as painful an eyesore as coal-burning stations, and not a wisp of smoke was in sight. When I began to ask questions, however, the company's public-relations man admitted that there are a few little problems. For one thing, the plant's innards are cooled with water pumped out of the Connecticut River. When it flows back in, this water raises the river's temperature by about twenty degrees, for a considerable distance. Apparently this had not yet done any serious damage to the shad, the only fish kept under surveillance; but its effect on other fish and algae, fish eggs, microorganisms, and the general ecology of the river is substantial though still unmeasured.

It would be possible, though expensive, for the company to build cooling towers, where the water would trickle over a series of baffles before returning to the river. In the process it would lose its heat to the atmosphere. But this, in turn, threatens climatic changes, such as banks of artificial fog rolling eastward over Long Island Sound, and serious wastage of water through evaporation from a river system where water already is in precarious supply. Moreover, neither this process nor any other now known would eliminate the slight, but not negligible, radiation which every atomic plant throws off, nor the remote but still omnipresent chance of a nuclear accident which could take thousands of lives. The building of an additional twenty plants along the banks of the Connecticut—which some estimates call for, in order to meet future demand for electricity—would be a clear invitation to an ecological disaster.

In the end I began to suspect that there is no harmless way to meet the demands for power of a rising population, with rising living standards—much less for a new herd of millions of electric cars. Every additional kilowatt levies some tax upon the environment, in one form or another. The Fourth Law of Thermodynamics seems to be: "There is no free lunch."

Everytime you look at one of the marvels of modern technology, you find a by-product—unintended, unpredictable, and often lethal. Since World War II American agriculture has performed miracles in increasing production. One result was that we were able for years to send a shipload of free wheat every day to India, saving millions from starvation. The by-products were: (1) a steady rise in India's population; (2) the poisoning of our streams and lakes with insecticides and chemical fertilizers; (3) the forced migration of some ten million people from the countryside to city slums, as agriculture became so efficient it no longer needed their labor.

Again, the jet plane is an unquestionable convenience, capable of whisking a New Yorker, say, to either the French Riviera or Southern California in a tenth of the time he could travel by ship or car, and at lower cost. But when he reaches his destination, the passenger finds the beaches coated with oil (intended to fuel planes, if it hadn't spilled) and the air thick with smog (thanks in good part to the jets, each of which spews out as much hydrocarbon as ten thousand automobiles).

Moreover, technology works best on things nobody really needs, such as collecting moon rocks or building supersonic transport planes. Whenever we try to apply it to something serious, it usually falls on its face.

An obvious case in point is the railroads. We already have the technology to build fast, comfortable passenger trains. Such trains are, in fact, already in operation in Japan, Italy, and a few other countries, Experimental samples—the Metroliners and Turbotrains—also are running with spectacular success between Washington and Boston. If we had enough of them to handle commuter and middle-distance traffic throughout the country, we could stop building the highways and airports which disfigure our countryside, reduce the number of automobiles contaminating the air, and solve many problems of urban congestion. But so far we have not been able to apply the relatively simple technology needed to accomplish these aims, because some tough political decisions have to be made before we can unleash the scientists and engineers. We would have to divert to the railroads many of the billions in subsidy which we now lavish on highways and air routes. We would have to get rid of our present railway management—in general, the most incompetent in American industry—and retire the doddering old codgers of the Railway Brotherhoods who make such a mess out of running our trains. This might mean public ownership of a good many rail lines. It certainly would mean all-out war with the unions, the auto and aviation industries, and the highway lobby. It would mean ruthless application of the No Growth principle to roads, cars, and planes, while we make sensible use instead of something we already have: some 20,000 miles of railways.

All this requires political action, of the most radical

kind. Until our Great Slob Society is willing to take it, technology is helpless.[7]

*(to be continued)*

*Is technology the problem? Or is the problem merely aggravated by technology? Is man the master or the slave of his technology? How might he become its master? Is it possible to devise a technological strategy of doing more with less, rather than doing less with more?*

[7] Fisher, "How I Got Radicalized."

# Earth: A New Covenant

*The Age of Nations is past.*
*The task before us now,*
*if we would not perish,*
*is to build the earth.*

*—Teilhard de Chardin*

## Our Landlord Is a Softy

Scene: A pearly-lit executive suite. The Landlord, seated on a throne-like chair, is listening to the annual year-end report of his Chief Collection Agent, Mr. Gabriel.

Mr. Gabriel: And so, Sir, there's no question that you have a beautiful piece of property there, all right. Ah, the way the grass smells after a rain. The brilliance of a snowfield on a crisp morning. The softness of a desert in the moonlight. The way a sea fog creeps in—

The Landlord (sighing): Yes, yes, Gabriel, I know. But let's get down to the facts and figures. What about depreciation this past year?

Mr. Gabriel (shaking his head): Not so good, Sir. They've burned some more holes in Vietnam . . . and frayed the Arab-Israeli border rather badly.

The Landlord: Just write it off under "Normal Wear and Tear," Gabriel.

Mr. Gabriel (dubiously): Well, if you say so, Sir. But what about the air?

The Landlord: Well, what about the air?

Mr. Gabriel (consulting notes): They've poured another 16.2 million tons of exhaust fumes, industrial smoke and other garbage into the air, Sir. Really, it's rapidly lowering the value of the entire property. (grudgingly) Of course, I will say they didn't make it as radioactive as they did the year before.

The Landlord (nodding): See? That's an encouraging note.

Mr. Gabriel: But it's a different story with the water supply.

The Landlord (sadly): I suppose it is.

Mr. Gabriel: Yes, they've dumped 13.2 trillion more gallons of sewage, mud, industrial chemicals and other poisons into virtually every rivulet, creek and river.

You cannot lie on your belly and drink from a cool, clear stream any more without chancing typhus, hepatitis, cholera. . . .

The Landlord (holding up his hand): Please, how were crops? I assume they've been growing things.

Mr. Gabriel: Yes. I was going to get to soil erosion next. During the past 12 months no less that 82.5 billion tons of rich loam . . .

The Landlord (hastily): But they have been improving the property, I'm sure. What about new construction?

Mr. Gabriel: Yes. Let's see, they have built 112,232 new public buildings, all of which they claim will look very nice. Once the trees grow. They have also erected 27,342 new oil derricks on once-pleasant hillsides, paved over 43 alpine meadows with freeways and . . .

The Landlord (wincing): Not the alpine meadows!

Mr. Gabriel (relentlessly): Yes, the alpine meadows. And thanks to advances in rocketry, they reached new heights with their debris. While, at the same time, they have been busy drilling a deep hole into the earth. To see what's inside.

The Landlord: It's more curiosity than vandalism.

Mr. Gabriel: Sir, you must face facts. You have a beautiful piece of property and undesirable tenants. By any conceivable rule of property management, you have but one choice. (raising a golden horn to his lips) Shall I sound the eviction notice now?

The Landlord (hesitating): No. Let's extend their short-term lease for just one more year, Gabriel.

Mr. Gabriel: But you've been saying that for ages, Sir.

The Landlord (sighing deeply): I know, Gabriel. But I keep thinking that sooner or later they're going to stop acting as though they owned the place.[1]

[1] Arthur Hoppe, "Our Landlord Is a Softy," *San Francisco Chronicle*, December 29, 1964. Copyright 1964 Chronicle Publishing Company.

*Even if our Landlord's patience were infinite, might not our short-term lease be canceled by our action?*

## Private Property?

My final apostasy from the American Creed was loss of faith in private property. I am now persuaded that there no longer is such a thing as truly private property, at least in land. That was a luxury we could afford only when the continent was sparsely settled. Today the use a man makes of his land cannot be left to his private decision alone, since eventually it is bound to affect everybody else. This conclusion I reached in anguish, since I own a tiny patch of land and value its privacy above anything money can buy.

What radicalized me on this score was the Department of Agriculture and Dr. Ian McHarg [McHarg, *Design with Nature*]. From those dull volumes of statistics which the Department publishes from time to time, I discovered that usable land is fast becoming a scarce resource—and that we are wasting it with an almost criminal lack of foresight. Every year, more than a million acres of farm and forest land is being eaten up by highways, airports, reservoirs, and real-estate developments. The best, too, in most cases, since the rich, flat bottom lands are the most tempting to developers.

Since America is, for the moment, producing a surplus of many crops, this destruction of farmland has not yet caused much public alarm. But some day, not too far off, the rising curve of population and the falling curve of food-growing land inevitably are going to intersect. That is the day when we may begin to understand what hunger means.

Long before that, however, we may be gasping for

breath. For green plants are our only source of oxygen. They also are the great purifiers of the atmosphere, since in the process of photosynthesis they absorb carbon dioxide—an assignment which gets harder every day, as our chimneys and exhaust pipes spew out ever-bigger tonnage of carbon gases. This is a function not only of trees and grass, but also of the tiny microorganisms in the sea. Indeed, its phytoplankton produces some 70 percent of all the oxygen on which life depends. These are delicate little creatures, easily killed by the sewage, chemicals, and oil wastes which already are contaminating every ocean in the world. Nobody knows when the scale will tip: when there are no longer enough green growing things to preserve the finely balanced mixture of gases in the atmosphere, by absorbing carbon dioxide and generating oxygen. All we know is that man is pressing down hard on the lethal end of the scale.

The Survivable Society, if we are able to construct it, will no longer permit a farmer to convert his meadow into a parking lot any time he likes. He will have to understand that his quick profit may, quite literally, take the bread out of his grandchildren's mouths, and the oxygen from their lungs. For the same reasons, housing developments will not be located where they suit the whim of a real-estate speculator or even the convenience of the residents. They will have to go on those few carefully chosen sites where they will do the least damage to the landscape, and to the life-giving greenery which it supports. . . .

The current excitement about the environment will not come to much, I am afraid, unless it radicalizes millions of Americans. The conservative ideas put forth by President Nixon—spending a few billion for sewage-treatment plans and abatement of air pollution—will not even begin to create the Survivable Society. That can be brought about only by radical political action—radical enough to change the whole structure of government, the economy, and our national goals.

How the Survivable State will work is something I cannot guess; its design is a job for the coming generation of political scientists. The radical vision can, however, give us a glimpse of what it might look like. It will measure every new law, every dollar of investment by a cardinal yardstick: Will this help us to accomplish a zero rate of growth and a stabilized environment? It will be skeptical of technology, including those inventions which purport to help clean up our earthly mess. Accordingly it will have an Anti-Patent Office, which will forbid the use of any technological discovery until the Office figures out fairly precisely what its side effects might be. (If they can't be foreseen, then the invention goes into deep freeze.) The use of land, water, and air will not be left to private decision, since their preservation will be recognized as a public trust.[2]

*Was there ever such a thing as truly private property? Can we lay personal claim to resources created by God, and at the same time avoid the state of separation which Christianity identifies as sin?*

*The earth lies polluted*
*under its inhabitants;*
*for they have transgressed the laws,*
*violated the statutes,*
*broken the everlasting covenant.*

—Isaiah 24:5

[2] Fisher, "How I Got Radicalized."

# A Tenet for Tenants

> *"Do they not understand that as man subdues nature he subdues himself—that man, being an animal, is as dependent upon the operation of natural laws as an amoeba or a frog?"*
>
> —Rienow, *Moment in the Sun*

Fundamental to the Judeo-Christian faith is the covenant relationship established between God and man. The covenant is an agreement between the Creator and the creature founded in mutual trust and faithfulness that each party in the relationship will fulfill his responsibilities.

The biblical records indicate that God is the Being who initiates the covenant and calls man into a unique relationship with him. Man's relationship with the Holy God is much more profound than a legal contract between two businessmen. A legal contract ceases to exist at a certain point in time—namely when each person has fulfilled the obligatory conditions of the agreement.

The *covenant* in both the Old and New Testaments is not merely a contract between equals that will cease at some point in time. Covenantal theology is grounded in a conditioned *relationship* between the Eternal God and finite man. The covenant is not an agreement between equals, but is rather a relationship of trust between God and man.

The conditions of the biblical covenant are clear:

*"Now therefore, if you will obey my voice and keep my covenant, you shall be my own possession among all peoples; for all the earth is mine, and you shall be to me a kingdom of priests and a holy*

*nation. These are the words which you shall speak to the children of Israel." (Exodus 19:5-6.)*

Faithful obedience to the commandments of God is what he requires of his children. In return, his children will enter into an everlasting relationship of harmony with God's purpose for the world. No part of the world is beyond the concern of God.

This understanding of the covenant relationship rests upon a peculiar understanding of the nature of God. God is a purposive Being who acts in history. Though a transcendental Being who authored the existence of the world, he did not then flee to some distant depth of the universe.

God is immanent and immediately present in the life of the world. This is precisely what the Gospel of John communicates—"The word was made flesh." The *Word* became flesh because there is purpose and meaning in the created order. Teilhard de Chardin is correct when he affirms that purposive will is the "Omega, He towards whom all converges, [and] is concurrently He from whom all radiates. Impossible to place him as a focus at the summit of the universe, without at the same time diffusing his presence in the intimate heart of the smallest movement of evolution." [3]

As men discover the unity and balance of the earth, they perceive the reality of a purposive will. The systems of the earth are not products of a haphazard creation. Consider the human body as one example of the complex order of Creation. The human body is composed of about fifty trillion cells; each cell is a composite of a nucleus containing protoplasm, chromosomes, and genes capable

[3] Teilhard de Chardin, *Building the Earth* (New York: Avon Books, 1969), p. 83.

of reproducing themselves. The nervous system of the body with the brain as its control center is a magnificent system controlling subconscious and conscious behavior. Breathing is a subconscious act which we normally do not think about. The metabolic process of the body chemistry enables the digestion of food, growth, and physical maturation. All these basic body functions are carried out within the context of a fundamental physiological unity. The numerous systems of the body function in an amazing unity that facilitates the life process. Abuse of the human body through improper diet, rest, and exercise will upset the delicate balance of the body. Illness and final demise is the result unless corrective measures are employed to reestablish the balance necessary for health.

The thin layer of life-sustaining elements on the surface of our planet, the biosphere, is not unlike the human organism. Like the human body, it is a complex system of energy transformations which enable life to exist. Man in the name of progress and industrial technology is upsetting the ecological balance of the planet's life-support system. If we continue to abuse the biosphere, death of the planet (for all human purposes) will become a reality.

The task of man is not to destroy the earth but to build it. Too often, building the earth has been equated with conquering nature. Man must cease to see nature as an object and perceive his being as a part of the total order and unity of the biosphere. Man is at one with the pulsating cycle of life. The becoming of nature is the becoming of man. The mysterious movement of nature from birth, through life, to death, and to rebirth is the covenant that man has with the earth. If man is to survive, he must live within the conditions of his covenant with the earth. This covenant is one in which man can trust nature to sustain his life and health, but only if man remains faithful to the *trust placed in him.* Otherwise, the covenant will be broken with disastrous consequences.

Man has *always* lived in a covenant with the earth, but he has lost sight of this in his obsession to subdue it and have dominion over all living things.

Because of this obsession, man breaks the covenant by viewing himself as an independent agent who rearranges the world for his own limited purposes. Man, through scientific and technological progress, has increased his material standard of living, extended his life expectancy, and created in himself the illusion that he owns the earth and is not accountable for the trust granted to him. Violation of this trust has taken the form of man's overloading the earth's systems beyond their natural capacity to function. At present the earth is like a 120-volt electrical system being subjected to a 220-volt charge.

We have reached a point of decision. What is required of us when we understand the ecological crisis is a commitment to radically change our own behavior. Man's covenant with the earth requires an ethic rooted fundamentally in *feeling for the earth.* "It is not our heads or our bodies which we must bring together but our hearts." [4] Perhaps we will first have to *feel* our way to ecological sanity before we have the commitment necessary to *think* and *act* to restore the integrity of the earth.

We are free to create a new world, but we do not have much time. Our earth ethic must be grounded in concern for all creation.

The Gospel of John says, "For God so loved the world that he gave his only Son" (3:16). In Genesis we read, "God saw everything that he had made, and behold, it

[4] *Ibid.*, p. 111.

was very good" (1:31). God *loves the world.* If man loves God, can he avoid loving the world?

*Care* must become the essential element of our earth ethic. An ethic grounded in care for the earth will become manifest when every scientific and technological resource is used to serve the order and balance of the earth.

Scientists tell us that the elements required to enable and sustain life as we know it came together billions of years ago to form the sun and its planets. About two million years ago man appeared in the evolutionary process. He has since evolved to become the dominant species. All other creatures live by his sufferance. This thrusts upon him the obligation to become the conscious intelligence of the planet.

Having taken command of the planet, man can no longer ignore the *first law* of the covenant: to have dominion over the earth, we must learn to obey her laws.

*How might you reestablish your covenant with the earth? List the ways in which you contribute to the violation of the planet.*

## Ten Commandments of the New Earth

1. You shall live in harmony with all the earth and with every living thing.
2. You shall have your fair share of the earth and no more.
3. You shall fight to protect the earth; it is your home.
4. You shall return to the earth all the organic treasures she freely gives you.
5. You shall make beautiful and enduring whatever is to be made.

6. You shall keep faith with future generations and be wise guardians of their inheritance.
7. You shall place necessity above greed, and wonder above wealth.
8. You shall trade only for necessary things, and demand no useless ones.
9. You shall be masters of technology and not its servants.
10. You shall come together with all your brothers and sisters and sing the joy of earth.[5]

## WILL Man Care for the Earth?

*"What man of you, if his son*
*asks him for a loaf, will give him*
*a stone? Or if he asks for a fish,*
*will give him a serpent? If you then,*
*who are evil, know how to give good*
*gifts to your children, how much more*
*will your Father who is in heaven give*
*good things to those who ask him?"*

(Matthew 7:9-11)

Some four and a half billion years of Creation have been invested in our planet's becoming a loaf rather than a stone. Given the tendency of the Creation to evolve matter from simple to complex forms, given the earth as the most complex celestial body known to us, and given ourselves as the most complex form to have evolved from the earth, we must conclude that our por-

[5] Adapted from the Commandments of the New Earth, composed by the Environmental Teach-In Committee of Milwaukee, Wisconsin.

tion of the Creation has so far been eminently successful. The question facing us now is whether we will sufficiently master our own complexity along with that of our spaceship to assure our continued success. Will we become whole men in time to preserve a whole earth?

If we truly have faith in the Creator and the Creation, there is no question as to whether we *can* care for the earth. We must, in that faith, assume that the Creation has evolved within us the potential to accept the responsibility it has placed upon us.

The ultimate question facing mankind today, therefore, is a question of will. *Will* we choose to care for the earth? *Will* we choose to become world-problem-solvers?

More specifically, will *you* choose to become a world problem-solver? Before you disqualify yourself, consider the following:

> We can all continue to say we are only churchmen, or only educators, or only students, or only government people—that our role is limited, and that we cannot be expected to solve the problems of the world. But the job of world-problem-solvers has not yet been allocated. Some of us had better choose to define ourselves as world-problem-solvers if world problems are going to be solved.[6]

What one thing can you do *as an individual* to serve the order and balance of the earth? What one thing can you do *in concert with others* to restore the integrity of the earth? (See the Bibliography section titled "Action Literature.")

[6] Robert Theobald, *An Alternative Future for America II* (Chicago, Swallow Press, 1970), pp. 53-54.

# Bibliography

All *books* below are available from your local bookstore or from All and Everything, Ltd., Whole Earth Store, 530 Dempster, Evanston, Ill. 60202.

## Action Literature

*Crisis in America: Hope through Action.* New York: National Council of Churches/Friendship Press, 1968.

*Environmental Action* (periodical). 2000 P St., N.W., Washington, D.C. 20036.

Hunter, Beatrice T. *Gardening Without Poisons.* Boston: Houghton Mifflin, 1964.

Mitchell, John G., and Stallings, Constance L., eds. *Ecotactics: The Sierra Club Handbook for Environmental Activists.* New York: Pocket Books, 1970.

*Rodale's Environmental Action Bulletin: Weekly Coverage of Health and Human Ecology News* (periodical). 33 E. Minor St., Emmaus, Pa. 18049.

*Vocations for Social Change* (periodical). Canyon, Calif. 94516.

## Alternative Futures

Boulding, Kenneth E. *The Meaning of the 20th Century.* New York: Harper & Row, 1964.

Brown, Harrison. *The Challenge of Man's Future.* New York: Viking Press, 1954.
Doxiadis, Constantinos A., and Douglass, Truman B. *The New World of Urban Man.* Philadelphia: United Church Press, 1965.
Drucker, Peter F. *Landmarks of Tomorrow.* New York: Harper & Row, 1959.
Ewald, William R., Jr., ed. *Environment and Change.* Bloomington: Indiana University Press, 1968.
———. *Environment and Policy.* Bloomington: Indiana University Press, 1968.
———. *Environment for Man.* Bloomington: Indiana University Press, 1967.
Fabun, Don. *The Dynamics of Change.* Englewood Cliffs, N.J.: Prentice-Hall, 1967.
*The Futurist* (periodical). World Future Society, P.O. Box 19285, Twentieth Street Station, Washington, D.C. 20036.
*The Green Revolution* (periodical). Heathcote Center, School of Living, Rt. 1, Box 129, Freeland, Md. 21053.
Hubbard, Earl. *The Search Is On.* Los Angeles: Pace Publications, 1969.
McHale, John. *The Future of the Future.* New York: Braziller, 1969.
*The Modern Utopian* (periodical). Alternatives Foundation, P.O. Box 1264, Berkeley, Calif. 94701.
Platt, John R. *The Step to Man.* New York: John Wiley, 1966.
Theobald, Robert. *An Alternative Future for America II.* Chicago: Swallow Press, 1970.
———, ed. *Committed Spending: A Route to Economic Security.* New York: Doubleday, 1968.
———, ed. *Guaranteed Income: Next Step in Economic Revolution.* New York: Doubleday, 1966.
———, ed. *Social Policies for America in the Seventies: Nine Divergent Views.* New York: Doubleday, 1968.
Whyte, Lancelot L. *The Next Development in Man.* New York: Mentor Books, 1946.
Wogaman, Philip. *Guaranteed Annual Income: The Moral Issues.* Nashville: Abingdon Press, 1968.

## Crisis Literature

Asimov, Isaac. "The Cancer Called Man." *Midwest Magazine,* June 14, 1970.

Borgstrum, Georg. *The Hungry Planet.* New York: Macmillan, 1965.
———. *Too Many: A Study of Earth's Biological Limitation.* New York: Macmillan, 1969.
Carson, Rachel. *Silent Spring.* Boston: Houghton Mifflin, 1962.
Cole, LaMont C. "Can the World Be Saved?" *BioScience,* July, 1968.
Commoner, Barry. *Science and Survival.* New York: Viking Press, 1966.
De Bell, Garrett, ed. *The Environmental Handbook.* New York: Ballantine Books, 1970.
*Earth Read Out* (periodical). 439 Boynton, Berkeley, Calif. 94707.
*Eco-Catastrophe,* by the editors of *Ramparts.* San Francisco: Canfield Press, 1970.
Ehrlich, Paul. *The Population Bomb.* New York: Ballantine Books, 1968.
*The Environment,* by the editors of *Fortune.* New York: Harper & Row, 1969.
*Environment* (periodical). Committee for Environmental Information, 438 N. Skinker Blvd., St. Louis, Mo. 63130.
Esposito, John C. *Vanishing Air.* New York: Grossman, 1970.
Fisher, John. "How I Got Radicalized: The Making of an Agitator for Zero." *Harper's Magazine,* April, 1970.
Graham, Frank. *Since Silent Spring.* Boston: Houghton Mifflin, 1970.
Kotulak, Ronald. "Is Man His Own Doomsday Machine?" *Chicago Tribune Magazine,* March 30, 1969.
Marine, Gene. *America the Raped.* New York: Simon & Schuster, 1969.
Marx, Wesley, *The Frail Ocean.* New York: Ballantine Books, 1970.
*The Mother Earth News* (periodical). Box 38, Madison, Ohio 44057.
Ng, Larry K. Y., and Mudd, Stuart. *The Population Crisis.* Bloomington: Indiana University Press, 1965.
Osborn, Fairfield. *Our Plundered Planet.* Boston: Little, Brown, 1948.
Paddock, William and Paul. *Famine 1975.* Boston: Little, Brown, 1968.
Rienow, Robert and Leona Train. *Moment in the Sun.* New York: Ballantine Books, 1967.
Rudd, Robert L. *Pesticides and the Living Landscape.* Madison: University of Wisconsin Press, 1964.
Taylor, Gordon Rattray. *The Doomsday Book.* New York: World, 1970.
———. "The Threat to Life in the Sea," *Saturday Review of Literature,* August 1, 1970.

Toffler, Alvin. *Future Shock*. New York: Random House, 1970.
Turner, James S. *The Chemical Feast*. New York: Grossman, 1970.

## Ecological Awareness

Bates, Marston. *Man in Nature*. 2nd. ed. Englewood Cliffs, N.J.: Prentice-Hall, 1964.

Bradbury, Ray. *The Golden Apples of the Sun*. New York: Bantam Books, 1961.

Charter, S. P. R. *For unto Us a Child Is Born*. San Francisco: Applegate Books, 1966.

———. *Man on Earth*. New York: Grove Press, 1970.

Ehrlich, Paul R. and Anne H. *Population, Resources, Environment: Issues in Human Ecology*. San Francisco: W. M. Freeman, 1970.

Hall, Edward T. *The Hidden Dimension*. New York: Doubleday, 1966.

Hardin, Garrett. *Population, Evolution, and Birth Control*. San Francisco: William Freeman, 1969.

Kormondy, Edward J. *Concepts of Ecology*. Englewood Cliffs, N.J.: Prentice-Hall, 1969.

McHarg, Ian L. *Design with Nature*. New York: The Natural History Press, 1969.

McKinley, Daniel, and Shepard, Paul, eds. *The Subversive Science, Essays Toward an Ecology of Man*. Boston: Houghton Mifflin, 1969.

Odum, Eugene P. *Ecology*. New York: Holt, Rinehart & Winston, 1963.

Storer, John H. *Man in the Web of Life*. New York: Signet Books, 1968.

———. *The Web of Life*. New York: Signet Books, 1953.

Wagner, Philip. *The Human Use of the Earth*. New York: The Free Press, 1960.

Young, Louise B., ed. *Population in Perspective*. New York: Oxford University Press, 1968.

## Films

*Choice: The Imperative of Tomorrow* (a series of four films):

1. "Creation or Destruction?" Raises the question of man's present ability to choose between unlimited destructive power or unlimited constructive power.

| | |
|---|---|
| 2. "Superman or Cyborg?" | Raises questions dealing with man's emerging ability to alter his own genetic and social evolution. |
| 3. "Preparation or Panic?" | Raises questions concerning the adequacy of our present educational systems for the type of life and choices which our youth will have to make. |
| 4. "The Need to Choose" | Raises the question of citizen participation in the processes of deciding the issues raised in earlier films. |

The Board of Laity, The United Methodist Church, 1200 Davis St., Evanston, Ill. 60201.

*DDT: Knowing It Survives Us.* Peter Robeck & Co., Inc., 230 Park Ave., New York, N.Y. 10017.

*The Idea of the City,* with John Kenneth Galbraith. University-at-Large, 70 West 40th St., New York, N.Y. 10018.

*Multiply and Subdue the Earth.* Audio-Visual Center, Indiana University, Bloomington, Ind. 47401.

*The River.* National Audio-visual Center, National Archives and Records Service, Washington, D.C. 20409.

*The Time of Man.* American Museum of Natural History, Central Park West at 79th St., New York, N.Y. 10024.

*What Do You Say When the Earth Is Dying?* Center for Curriculum Design, 823 Foster St., Evanston, Ill. 60204.

*Who Killed Lake Erie?* University of Michigan, Audio Visual Education Center, 416 Fourth St., Ann Arbor, Mich. 48103.

## The Human Condition

Berrill, N. J. *Inherit the Earth.* New York: Fawcett Premier Books, 1967.

Dubos, Rene. *So Human an Animal.* New York: Scribner's, 1968.

Molton, Warren Lane. *Bruised Reeds,* Valley Forge, Pa.: Judson Press, 1970.

Montagu, Ashley. *The Direction of Human Development.* New York: Hawthorn Books, 1970.

Morris, Desmond. *The Human Zoo.* New York: McGraw-Hill, 1969.

## Resource Materials

*Ecologos* (A Reading List). Sidney Kramer Books, 1722 H St. N.W., Washington, D.C. 20006.

*The Whole Earth Catalog*. Portola Institute, 558 Santa Cruz Ave., Menlo Park, Calif. 94025.

*The World Game*, Box 909, Carbondale, Ill. 60921.

## Spaceship Earth

Boulding, Kenneth E. "Economics of the Coming Spaceship Earth," in Garrett De Bell, ed., *The Environmental Handbook*. New York: Ballantine Books, 1970.

———, and Clark, Henry. *Human Values on the Spaceship Earth*. New York: National Council of Churches/Council Press, 1966.

Cole, LaMont C. "The Ecosphere." *Scientific American*, April, 1958.

Fuller, R. Buckminster. *An Operating Manual for Spaceship Earth*. New York: Pocket Books, 1970.

Pollard, William G. "The Earth as a Spaceship." *The Science Teacher*, September, 1969.

———. *Man on a Spaceship*. Claremont, Calif.: The Claremont Colleges, 1967.

Ward, Barbara. *Spaceship Earth*. New York: Columbia University Press, 1966.

## Technology

Burke, John G. *The New Technology and Human Values*. Belmont, Calif.: Wadsworth Publishing Co., 1966.

Doxiadis, Constantinos A. *Ekistics*. New York: Oxford University Press, 1968.

*Ekistics: Reviews on the Problems and Science of Human Settlements* (periodical). Athens Center of Ekistics, Box 471, Athens, Greece.

Ferkiss, Victor C. *Technological Man: The Myth and the Reality*. New York: Braziller, 1969.

Hall, Cameron P. *Human Values and Advancing Technology*. New York: National Council of Churches/Friendship Press, 1967.

Marks, Robert W. *The Dymaxion World of Buckminster Fuller*. Carbondale: Southern Illinois University Press, 1960.

Mumford, Lewis. *Technics and Civilization*. New York: Harcourt Brace Jovanovich, 1934, 1962.

Theobald, Robert, ed. *Dialogue on Technology*. Indianapolis: Bobbs-Merrill, 1967.

## Theology

Bonifazi, Conrad. *A Theology of Things.* Philadelphia: Lippincott, 1967.

*Christianity and Ecology: A Selected Bibliography.* Word, Inc., Box 1790, Waco, Tex. 76703 (mimeo).

*Christians and the Good Earth.* Faith, Man and Nature Group, 800 S. Royal Street, Alexandria, Va. 22314.

Cox, Harvey. *The Secular City.* New York: Macmillan, 1965.

Elder, Fredrick. *Crisis in Eden.* Nashville: Abingdon Press, 1970.

Rust, Eric C. *Science and Faith.* New York: Oxford University Press, 1967.

Sittler, Joseph. "A Theology for Earth." *The Christian Scholar,* June 1, 1954.

Teilhard de Chardin, Pierre. *Building the Earth.* New York: Avon Books, 1969.

White, Lynn, Jr. "The Historical Roots of Our Ecological Crisis," in Garrett De Bell, ed., *The Environmental Handbook.* New York: Ballantine Books, 1970.